1st EDITION

Perspectives on Diseases and Disorders

Traumatic Brain Injury

Arthur Gillard

Book Editor

PERSPECTIVES
On Diseases & Disorders

GALE
CENGAGE Learning·

Detroit • New York • San Francisco • New Haven, Conn • Waterville, Maine • London

Elizabeth Des Chenes, *Director, Publishing Solutions*

© 2014 Greenhaven Press, a part of Gale, Cengage Learning

WCN: 01-100-101

THE LIBRARY OF CONGRESS HAS CATALOGED THE EARLIER EDITION AS FOLLOWS:

Traumatic brain injury / Arthur Gillard, book editor.
   p. cm. -- (Perspectives on diseases and disorders)
   Summary: "Traumatic Brain Injury: Each volume in this timely series provides essential information on a disease or disorder (symptoms, causes, treatments, cures, etc.); presents the controversies surrounding causes, alternative treatments, and other issues"-- Provided by publisher.
  Includes bibliographical references and index.
  ISBN 978-0-7377-6349-2 (hardback)
 1. Brain damage. 2. Head--Wounds and injuries. I. Gillard, Arthur.
  RC387.5.T725 2012
  617.5'1044--dc23

                   2012015514

ISBN: 978-0-7377-7311-8

Printed in the United States of America
1 2 3 4 5 6 7 18 17 16 15 14

CONTENTS

   Every year many people sustain serious head injuries from sports, car accidents, and other causes. The nature of the trauma determines the type of brain damage that results, ranging from a mild concussion to very severe brain injury with serious long-term consequences.

   Advanced diagnostic techniques available today, such as computed tomography (CT), magnetic resonance imaging (MRI), and neuropsychological evaluation, have greatly enhanced the prospects for brain trauma patients, reducing the percentage of cases considered hopeless.

FOREWORD

"Medicine, to produce health, has to examine disease."
—Plutarch

Independent research on a health issue is often the first step to complement discussions with a physician. But locating accurate, well-organized, understandable medical information can be a challenge. A simple Internet search on terms such as "cancer" or "diabetes," for example, returns an intimidating number of results. Sifting through the results can be daunting, particularly when some of the information is inconsistent or even contradictory. The Greenhaven Press series Perspectives on Diseases and Disorders offers a solution to the often overwhelming nature of researching diseases and disorders.

From the clinical to the personal, titles in the Perspectives on Diseases and Disorders series provide students and other researchers with authoritative, accessible information in unique anthologies that include basic information about the disease or disorder, controversial aspects of diagnosis and treatment, and first-person accounts of those impacted by the disease. The result is a well-rounded combination of primary and secondary sources that, together, provide the reader with a better understanding of the disease or disorder.

Each volume in Perspectives on Diseases and Disorders explores a particular disease or disorder in detail. Material for each volume is carefully selected from a wide range of sources, including encyclopedias, journals, newspapers, nonfiction books, speeches, government documents, pamphlets, organization newsletters, and position papers. Articles in the first chapter provide an authoritative, up-to-date overview that covers symptoms, causes and effects, treatments, cures, and medical advances. The second chapter presents a substantial number of opposing viewpoints on controversial treatments and other current debates relating to the volume topic. The third chapter offers a variety of personal perspectives on the disease or disorder. Patients, doctors, caregivers, and loved ones represent just some of the voices found in this narrative chapter.

Each Perspectives on Diseases and Disorders volume also includes:

- An **annotated table of contents** that provides a brief summary of each article in the volume.
- An **introduction** specific to the volume topic.
- Full-color **charts and graphs** to illustrate key points, concepts, and theories.
- Full-color **photos** that show aspects of the disease or disorder and enhance textual material.
- **"Fast Facts"** that highlight pertinent additional statistics and surprising points.
- A **glossary** providing users with definitions of important terms.
- A **chronology** of important dates relating to the disease or disorder.
- An annotated list of **organizations to contact** for students and other readers seeking additional information.
- A **bibliography** of additional books and periodicals for further research.
- A detailed **subject index** that allows readers to quickly find the information they need.

Whether a student researching a disorder, a patient recently diagnosed with a disease, or an individual who simply wants to learn more about a particular disease or disorder, a reader who turns to Perspectives on Diseases and Disorders will find a wealth of information in each volume that offers not only basic information, but also vigorous debate from multiple perspectives.

INTRODUCTION

Saturday, January 8, 2011, started out as an ordinary day for congresswoman Gabrielle Giffords. Only a few days before, she had decided to hold a "Congress on Your Corner" event to meet with her constituents at a local Safeway supermarket in Arizona. Just moments after the event began, a mentally ill man shot her at close range, then fired another twenty-nine bullets randomly into the crowd. The first bullet hit Giffords above her left eye, tearing through the left hemisphere of her brain at one thousand feet per second, causing severe brain damage and changing her life forever. Her community outreach director, Gabe Zimmerman, was also shot in the head a short distance from her, and—like about 90 percent of people shot in the head—died from his injury. Giffords was lucky to survive, but her ordeal was just beginning.

The Centers for Disease Control and Prevention (CDC) estimates that each year in the United States, 1.7 million people experience a traumatic brain injury (TBI). Eighty percent, or 1.4 million, receive treatment in an emergency room and are then released. Of these, 275,000 cases are considered serious enough to require hospitalization, and 52,000 TBI incidents result in death. Each year 80,000–90,000 people are permanently disabled by a TBI. Brain injury case manager Michael Paul Mason puts the statistics in perspective this way: "In America alone, so many people become permanently disabled from a brain injury that each decade they could fill a city the size of Detroit. Seven of these cities arc filled already. A third of their citizens are under fourteen years of age."[1]

High-profile cases like that of Giffords, as well as an increasing number of media reports about the damage done by concussions in both amateur and professional sports—including a serious degenerative disease called chronic traumatic encephalopathy (CTE), which can affect athletes who have suffered multiple concussions during their careers—have done much to raise public awareness of TBI in recent years. In addition, TBI has been recognized as a "signature wound" of the wars in Afghanistan and Iraq. The Pentagon and the Rand Corporation have independently estimated that more than 300,000 veterans of those wars may have suffered brain injury, mainly from improvised explosive devices (IEDs).

Common causes of TBI in the United States include falls (35 percent), motor vehicle accidents (17 percent), and assaults (10 percent). However it happens, the effects of brain injury are as individual as those who suffer them. As TBI survivor and author Garry Prowe writes:

> Every brain injury varies in the type, location, and extent of the damage suffered. Consequently, each survivor acquires a unique mix of symptoms. One person, for example, may need a cane to compensate for her shaky balance and the patience of others to comprehend her slurred speech. A second survivor may display no physical complaints, but explodes with anger when asked to take out the garbage. She also strikes up long, one-sided conversations with strangers. A third person may be unable to find the right word in conversation and becomes agitated in public places. She just wants to be left alone to play video games in her room. A fourth survivor may display no outward signs of an injury, but has subtle lapses of concentration and information processing, which only those closest to her can recognize.[2]

In Giffords's case, she was left with persistent deficits such as right-side weakness and neglect (often survivors of significant brain injury will neglect or ignore

the side of their body opposite to the site of the injury because they have little or no awareness of it), problems concentrating and remembering, and a disorder known as aphasia, which severely compromises her ability to communicate. Her husband, Mark Giffords, notes that after the injury, she got tired very easily (typical of people recovering from TBI) and also observed that "since the shooting, her emotions often seemed magnified. When she was happy, she was really happy. When she was sad, she could get very sad."[3]

Gabrielle Giffords returned to Congress to an emotional welcome on January 24, 2012. She is greeted here by President Barack Obama before his State of the Union speech. (© AP Images/ Martin H. Simon/Corbis)

For people with severe brain injury, the subjective effects in some cases can be quite profound and disorienting, as science writer Bruce Bower describes:

> The concept of identity theft assumes an entirely new meaning for people with brain injuries that rob them of their sense of self—the unspoken certainty that one exists as a person in a flesh-bounded body with a unique set of life experiences and relationships. Consider the man who, after sustaining serious brain damage, insisted that his parents, siblings, and friends had been replaced by look-alikes whom he had never met. Everyone close to him had become a familiar-looking stranger. Another brain-injured patient asserted that his physicians, nurses, and physical therapists were actually his sons, daughters-in-law, and coworkers. He identified himself as an ice skater whom he had seen on a television program.[4]

Luckily for Giffords, her personality, memory, and sense of self were largely intact. Nevertheless, she had a long road of recovery ahead of her. Initially she was placed in a medically induced coma for several days to give her brain a chance to heal. A large section of her skull was removed to prevent further damage as the injured tissues of her brain swelled. Once her condition had stabilized, her rehabilitation began—hours of intense speech and physical therapy almost every day for many months. For some time after the accident, she could not speak at all, and she felt—as she later reported—like a "zombie." In the time since her injury, she has recovered to an impressive degree, but still has a long way to go in her rehabilitation process. Recovery from traumatic brain injury is an open-ended and life-long process. As Debbie Hampton, herself a brain injury survivor, observes from personal experience, "Recovering from a brain injury is not pretty. It is grueling, hard work, for sure, but with determined, persistent effort—

and, I mean every day, for years—anything is possible."[5] Stephan Mayer, professor of neurology and neurological surgery at Columbia University, is "still amazed from time to time at how well people do, and I think that we have simply underestimated the resilience and regenerative capacity in the human brain."[6]

With so much research and attention being focused on TBI these days, the potential for healing and recovery is getting better all the time. Rehabilitation techniques being explored by researchers include stem cells, transcranial magnetic stimulation, electrodes, antidepressants, and induced hypothermia. But while treatment and rehabilitation services continue to improve, at the present time not everyone has equal access to the resources that are available. Giffords was lucky to receive top-notch care, which, in addition to her determination and indomitable spirit, helped her to recover to an astonishing degree from her injury. Yet many others are not so fortunate. Michael Paul Mason notes that "in today's healthcare system . . . most TBI survivors now average a stay of thirty days in rehab. . . . For all the limitless potential of technological advances, we live with, and permit, a highly limited level of healthcare, and nowhere is this disparity more vivid than in the lives of brain-injured individuals."[7]

Perspectives on Diseases and Disorders: Traumatic Brain Injury provides an accessible overview of a challenging health condition. Incorporating the perspectives of experts, health care providers, and TBI sufferers themselves, this volume provides opportunities to enhance awareness about an often unacknowledged medical condition.

Notes

1. Michael Paul Mason, *Head Cases: Stories of Brain Injury and Its Aftermath.* New York: Farrar, Straus & Giroux, 2008, pp. 7–8.

2. Garry Prowe, *Successfully Surviving a Brain Injury: A Family Guidebook; From the Emergency Room to Selecting a Rehabilitation Facility.* Gainesville, FL: Brain Injury Success, 2010, p. 20.

3. Quoted in Gabrielle D. Giffords and Mark E. Kelly, *Gabby: A Story of Courage and Hope.* New York: Scribner, 2011, p. 259.

4. Bruce Bower, "Self-Serve Brains: Personal Identity Veers to the Right Hemisphere," *Science News,* February 11, 2006. http://biopsychiatry.com/misc/personal-identity.html.

5. Debbie Hampton, "The Better It Gets, the Better It Gets," The Best Brain Possible, November 17, 2011. www.thebestbrainpossible.com/the-better-it-gets-the-better-it-gets.

6. Quoted in Elizabeth Landau, "The Brain's Amazing Potential for Recovery," CNN, May 5, 2011. www.cnn.com/2011/HEALTH/05/05/brain.plasticity.giffords/index.html.

7. Mason, *Head Cases,* pp. 95–96.

CHAPTER 1

Understanding Traumatic Brain Injury

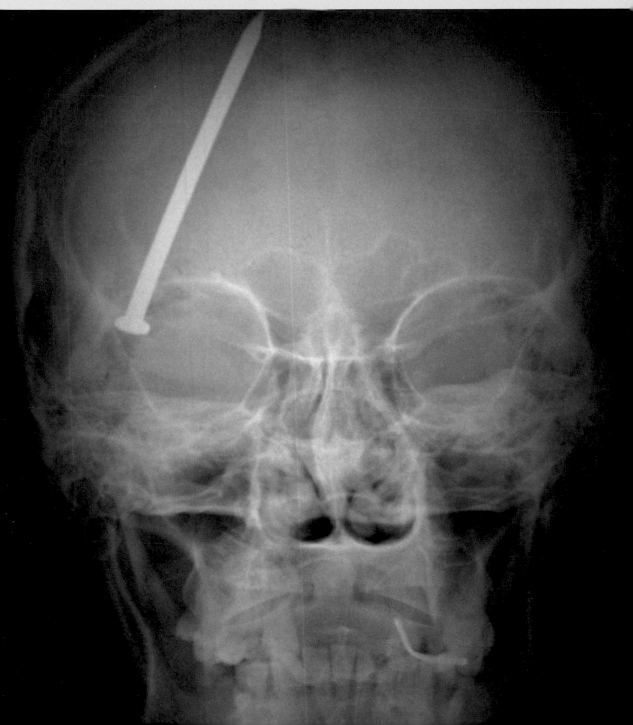

An Overview of Traumatic Brain Injury

Laura Jean Cataldo et al.

In the following viewpoint, the authors describe a variety of ways in which injury to the head can result in traumatic brain injury (TBI), and the types of injury that can result. The authors note that up to 750,000 people in the United States each year sustain a brain injury severe enough to need hospitalization. According to the authors, causes of such injury include traffic accidents, sports injuries, falls, workplace accidents, assaults, or bullets. Mechanisms of damage to the brain as a result of closed or penetrating head injury are described, such as bleeding, blood clots, and nerve fiber tearing from the brain swirling around in the head. The authors list symptoms for each type of injury and distinguish between mild and severe brain trauma.

Photo on previous page. Brain trauma can range from mild concussion to severe brain injury with long-term consequences such as with this patient, whose penetrating head injury resulted from a lodged nail. (© Robert Destefano/ Alamy)

Injury to the head may damage the scalp, skull, or brain. The most important consequence of head trauma is traumatic brain injury. Head injury may occur either as a closed head injury, such as the head hitting a car's windshield, or as a penetrating head injury, as

SOURCE: Laura Jean Cataldo et. al., "Head Injury," *The Gale Encyclopedia of Medicine*, 4E, 2011, Cengage Learning. All rights reserved. Reproduced by permission.

when a bullet pierces the skull. Both may cause damage that ranges from mild to profound. Very severe injury can be fatal because of profound brain damage.

Most people have had some type of head injury at least once in their lives, but rarely do they require a hospital visit. Each year about two million people in the United States have a serious head injury, and up to 750,000 of them are severe enough to require hospitalization. Brain injury is most likely to occur in males between the ages of 15 and 24 years, usually because of car and motorcycle accidents. About 70% of all accidental deaths are due to head injuries, as are most of the disabilities that occur after trauma.

Types and Symptoms of Brain Trauma

External trauma to the head is capable of damaging the brain, even if there is no external evidence of damage. More serious injuries can cause skull fracture, blood clots between the skull and the brain, or bruising and tearing of the brain tissue itself.

Injuries to the head can be caused by traffic accidents, sports injuries, falls, workplace accidents, assaults, or bullets.

A person who has had a head injury and who is experiencing the following symptoms should seek medical care immediately:

- serious bleeding from the head or face
- loss of consciousness, however brief
- confusion and lethargy
- lack of pulse or breathing
- clear fluid drainage from the nose or ear.

Direct and Secondary Damage to the Brain

A head injury may cause damage both from the direct physical injury to the brain and from secondary factors, such as lack of oxygen, brain swelling, and disturbance

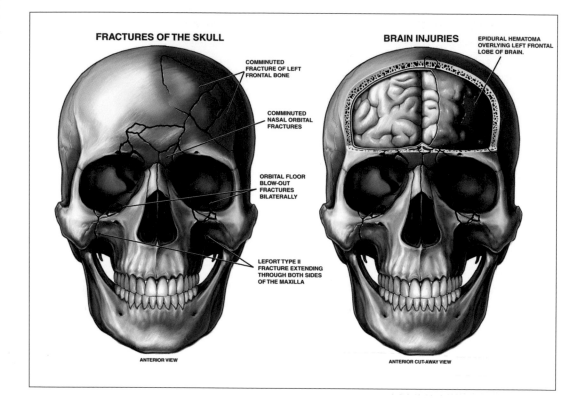

FRACTURES OF THE SKULL

COMMINUTED
FRACTURE OF LEFT
FRONTAL BONE

COMMINUTED
NASAL ORBITAL
FRACTURES

ORBITAL FLOOR
BLOW-OUT
FRACTURES
BILATERALLY

LEFORT TYPE II
FRACTURE EXTENDING
THROUGH BOTH SIDES
OF THE MAXILLA

ANTERIOR VIEW

BRAIN INJURIES

EPIDURAL HEMATOMA
OVERLYING LEFT FRONTAL
LOBE OF BRAIN.

ANTERIOR CUT-AWAY VIEW

This illustration depicts skull fractures, left, and subsequent hematoma of the brain as a result of the fractures. (© Nucleus Medical Art, Inc./Alamy)

of blood flow. Both closed and penetrating head injuries can cause swirling movements throughout the brain, tearing nerve fibers and causing widespread bleeding or a blood clot in or around the brain. Swelling may raise pressure within the skull (intracranial pressure) and may block the flow of oxygen to the brain.

Head trauma may cause a concussion, in which there is a brief loss of consciousness without visible structural damage to the brain. In addition to loss of consciousness, initial symptoms of brain injury may include:

- memory loss and confusion
- vomiting
- dizziness
- partial paralysis or numbness
- shock
- anxiety.

After a head injury, there may be a period of impaired consciousness followed by a period of confusion and impaired memory with disorientation and a breakdown in the ability to store and retrieve new information. Others experience temporary amnesia following head injury that begins with memory loss over a period of weeks, months, or years before the injury (retrograde amnesia). As the patient recovers, memory slowly returns. Post-traumatic amnesia refers to loss of memory for events during and after the accident.

Epilepsy occurs in 2–5% of people who have had a head injury; it is much more common in people who have had severe or penetrating injuries. Most cases of epilepsy appear right after the accident or within the first year, and become less likely with increased time following the accident.

Closed and Penetrating Head Injury

Closed head injury refers to brain injury without any penetrating injury to the brain. It may be the result of a direct blow to the head; of the moving head being rapidly stopped, such as when a person's head hits a windshield in a car accident; or by the sudden deceleration of the head without its striking another object. The kind of injury the brain receives in a closed head injury is determined by whether or not the head was unrestrained upon impact and the direction, force, and velocity of the blow. If the head is resting on impact, the maximum damage will be found at the impact site. A moving head will cause a "contrecoup injury" where the brain damage occurs on the side opposite the point of impact, as a result of the brain slamming into that side of the skull. A closed head injury also may occur without the head being struck, such as when a person experiences whiplash. This type of injury occurs because the brain is of a different density than

> **FAST FACT**
>
> According to a study published by the Massachusetts Medical Society in 2009, risk of epilepsy increases twofold following mild brain injury and sevenfold following severe brain injury.

the skull and can be injured when delicate brain tissues hit against the rough, jagged inner surface of the skull.

If the skull is fractured, bone fragments may be driven into the brain. Any object that penetrates the skull may implant foreign material and dirt into the brain, leading to an infection. A skull fracture is a medical emergency that must be treated promptly to prevent possible brain damage. Such an injury may be obvious if blood or bone fragments are visible, but it is possible for a fracture to have occurred without any apparent damage. A skull fracture should be suspected if there is:

- blood or clear fluid leaking from the nose or ears
- unequal pupil size
- bruises or discoloration around the eyes or behind the ears
- swelling or depression of part of the head.

Intracranial Bleeding and Hematomas

Bleeding (hemorrhage) inside the skull may accompany a head injury and cause additional damage to the brain. A blood clot (hematoma) may occur if a blood vessel between the skull and the brain ruptures; when the blood leaks out and forms a clot, it can press against brain tissue, causing symptoms from a few hours to a few weeks after the injury. If the clot is located between the bones of the skull and the covering of the brain (dura), it is called an epidural hematoma. If the clot is between the dura and the brain tissue itself, the condition is called a subdural hematoma. In other cases, bleeding may occur deeper inside the brain. This condition is called intracerebral hemorrhage or intracerebral contusion (from the word for bruising).

In any case, if the blood flow is not stopped, it can lead to unconsciousness and death. The symptoms of bleeding within the skull include:

- nausea and vomiting
- headache

- loss of consciousness
- unequal pupil size
- lethargy.

Post-Concussion Syndrome

If the head injury is mild, there may be no symptoms other than a slight headache. There also may be confusion, dizziness, and blurred vision. While the head injury may seem to have been quite mild, in many cases symptoms persist for days or weeks. Up to 60% of patients who sustain a mild brain injury continue to experience a range of symptoms called "post-concussion syndrome," as long as six months or a year after the injury.

The symptoms of post-concussion syndrome can result in a puzzling interplay of behavioral, cognitive, and emotional complaints that can be difficult to diagnose, including:

- headache
- dizziness
- mental confusion
- behavior changes
- memory loss
- cognitive deficits
- depression
- emotional outbursts.

Assessing the Extent of Damage

The extent of damage in a severe head injury can be assessed with computed tomography (CT) scans, magnetic resonance imaging (MRI) scans, positron emission tomography (PET) scans, electroencephalogram (EEG) recordings, and routine neurological and neuropsychological evaluations.

Doctors use the Glasgow Coma Scale to evaluate the extent of brain damage based on observing a patient's ability to open his or her eyes, respond verbally, and respond to stimulation by moving (motor response). Patients can score from three to 15 points on this scale. People who score

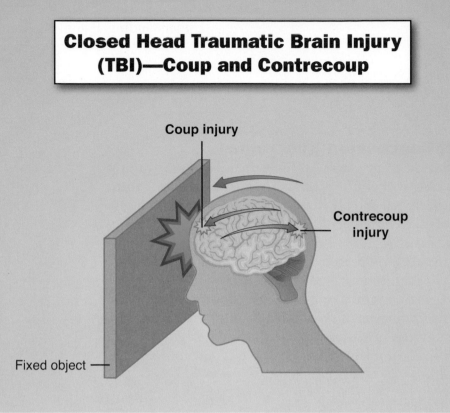

Closed Head Traumatic Brain Injury (TBI)—Coup and Contrecoup

Coup injury

Contrecoup injury

Fixed object

below eight when they are admitted usually have suffered a severe brain injury and will need rehabilitative therapy as they recover. In general, higher scores on the Glasgow Coma Scale indicate less severe brain injury and a better prognosis for recovery.

Patients with a mild head injury who experience symptoms are advised to seek out the care of a specialist; unless a family physician is thoroughly familiar with medical literature in this newly emerging area, experts warn that there is a good chance that patient complaints after a mild head injury will be downplayed or dismissed. . . .

Patients with continuing symptoms after a mild head injury should call a local chapter of a head-injury foundation that can refer patients to the best nearby expert.

If a concussion, bleeding inside the skull, or skull fracture is suspected, the patient should be kept quiet in a darkened room, with head and shoulders raised slightly on a pillow or blanket.

Advanced Diagnostic Techniques Are Used in Brain Injury Cases

John W. Cassidy

John W. Cassidy is a neuropsychiatrist and former Harvard Medical School faculty member who founded the traumatic brain injury program at Boston's McLean Hospital. In the following selection, Cassidy describes diagnostic tests used to determine the extent and nature of brain damage in patients with traumatic brain injury (TBI). According to the author, some tests—such as computed tomography (CT) or magnetic resonance imaging (MRI)—allow doctors or researchers to see whether brain tissue is healthy or damaged. Other tests, such as positron-emission tomography (PET) or electroencephalogram (EEG), can tell how regions of the brain are functioning. Whereas those tests provide objective measurements of brain structure or functioning, Cassidy explains that neuropsychological evaluation—in which a doctor attempts to understand how the patient is processing information—is more subjective in nature but helpful in determining whether a person suffering from TBI is able to return to work or school.

SOURCE: John W. Cassidy, *Mindstorms: The Complete Guide for Families Living with Traumatic Brain Injury.* New York: Da Capo Press. 2009, pp. 40–46. Copyright © 2009 by Da Capo Press. All rights reserved. Reproduced by permission.

Today's technology and treatment is light years ahead of applying leeches, but we still have a long way to go before we can say that we have conquered brain injury. Thanks to newer and better diagnostic techniques, the percentage of cases deemed hopeless has diminished.

Here, very briefly, are some of the diagnostic testing methods and technologies used in the evaluation of brain injury.

CT Scanning

Computed (or *computerized*) *tomography (CT)* scans have advanced our ability to see the visible results of brain injury. CT scans collect X rays that have passed through the body (those not absorbed by tissue) with an electronic detector mounted on a rotating frame rather than on film. The X-ray source and collector rotate around the patient as they emit and absorb X rays. Computers then combine the different readings, or views, of a patient's brain into a coherent picture usable for diagnosis.

During a CT scan, a patient lies inside a white, donut-shaped capsule as a technician takes 3-D pictures of "slices" of her brain. With each camera click, the tissues of the brain are peeled away, revealing problem areas not visible with a traditional X-ray machine. One important use for the CT scan occurs in the emergency room as technicians use it to detect bleeding in the brain.

Magnetic Resonance Imaging (MRI)

Combining imaging, physics, and computer technology, *magnetic resonance imaging (MRI)* is even better than CT scanning at looking at both the external and internal anatomy of the brain. Utilizing radio frequency pulses and magnets to image even small clusters of brain cells, MRI converts the resulting signals into a highly detailed picture of the brain, exposing minute details that, in the years before this test became available, would have gone undetected, especially in deep brain structures. However, these machines are more complicated to use than CT scanners and the test takes much longer to perform. Thus, they are not usually used to view the brain immediately following an accident. MRI data are better used in the days after the acute phases of the injury have subsided, when the immediate medical crisis has passed.

PET and SPECT Scans

These tests provide more than just anatomic information about the brain (that is, pictures of the brain structures). When an injected radioactive tracer flows through the brain and is transported inside of healthy brain cells, a *positron emission tomography (PET)* scan creates a map that can evaluate brain function, not just structure. Because it can show functional damage to the brain, it produces a different kind of data that can supplement the information gathered via the MRI technique. These scans let us know whether injured areas of the brain are continuing to function, rather than just giving us a picture showing whether they have been physically distorted or damaged.

> **FAST FACT**
>
> Diffusion tensor imaging, a new type of magnetic resonance imaging, detects abnormal water flow in nerve fibers, improving diagnosis in mild traumatic brain injury.

Single photon emission computed tomography (SPECT) is similar to the PET scan except that it uses a more standard and radioactively stable tracer that provides some evidence of brain dysfunction. It is not as specific as the PET scan in determining underlying brain functioning, but it is more readily available and less expensive than PET scanning. However, it is important to note that neither PET nor SPECT scanning are currently considered clinical tools in the standard practice of managing brain injury. They remain mostly experimental in nature. . . . As with many newer technologies, they are likely to be incorporated into standard practice to answer certain diagnostic questions in the future, but not just yet.

Electroencephalogram (EEG)

An *electroencephalogram* is similar to an electrocardio-gram (ECG or EKG), except that instead of measuring electrical impulses in the heart, it measures them in the brain via electrodes attached to the scalp. It is very important to remember that an EEG can record brain electrical activity only while the electrodes remain attached to the skull. We've all heard stories of people who, after being told by their doctor that they have "a perfectly normal EKG," drop dead from a heart attack the next day. Likewise, EEG readings show us only what is going on in the brain during the time the EEG is actively running; an EEG can miss rare events, and it certainly will not show future electrical abnormalities that have not yet occurred. Abnormal sharp waves, seen as episodic electrical peaks and valleys, or spikes on a printout, for example, may suggest an underlying seizure disorder, but usually clinical correlation is required to ensure a reliable diagnosis. In severe brain injury, background slowing is often seen on an EEG, suggesting underlying, diffuse brain dysfunction, but that does not provide a diagnosis of what is exactly wrong. It is also very important to remember that the diagnosis of an early disorder does not mean that it will persist. If it does, the diagnosis of epilepsy may be appropriate.

Evoked Potentials

Like EEGs, tests called *evoked potentials* measure electrical activity in the brain, but they take it one step further. This diagnostic tool involves provoking electrical impulses in the brain by means of visual, auditory, and sensory stimuli (in three different tests) to measure the brain's ability to respond. Once an appropriate stimulus has been provided to an area of the brain, the corresponding electrical response is recorded and evaluated so that the technician can determine whether that area of the brain is functioning as it should be electrically, compared with studies of the same stimulus being applied to the same brain area in uninjured individuals.

Neuropsychological Evaluation

In a neuropsychological evaluation the physician attempts to understand an individual's information processing system; that is, how he processes information from the world around him to make decisions and act

Glasgow Coma Scale

The Glasgow Coma Scale (GCS) is a test that measures the eye opening response, verbal response, and motor response of head injury patients to assess the level of consciousness and severity of the injury. The GCS score is the sum of the highest points from each category. The lower the score, the more severe the injury.

Points	Best Eye Function	Best Verbal Response	Best Motor Response
6	—	—	Follows commands with face, arms or legs
5	—	Oriented to name, place, and situation	Does not follow commands but exhibits purposeful movement
4	Opens eyes spontaneously	Appropriate speech but confused	Only withdraws to painful stimulus
3	Opens eyes to speech	Inappropriate speech but comprehensible words	Flexes (decorticate posturing) to painful stimulus
2	Opens eyes to pain	Sounds but no comprehensible words	Extends (decerebrate posturing) to painful stimulus
1	Does not open eyes to any stimulus	No sounds to any stimulus	No movement to any stimulus

Taken from: Rahul Jadial, Charles B. Newman, and Samuel A. Hughes. *100 Questions and Answers About Head and Brain Injuries*, 2009.

on them in daily life. There are two components to the information processing system. The first consists of the five basic cognitive processes: attention, incorporation, retention, synthesis, and execution. The second is directed at identifying the efficiency with which the basic processes function. Efficiency factors include speed, endurance, consistency, stress tolerance, and cognitive flexibility as well as psychological variables.

There are a multitude of standardized tests available to assess each aspect of the information processing system. The neuropsychologist selects those tests best suited to assessing the individual's abilities in each area. Issues considered in test selection include the individual's medical status, motor functioning, ability to communicate, and cultural background in an effort to eliminate

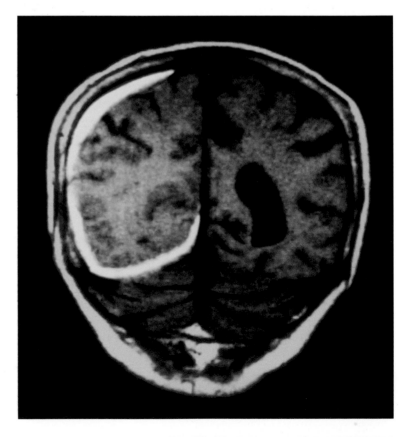

A magnetic resonance imaging (MRI) scan of a patient's brain shows subdural hematoma on the left side. MRIs are instrumental in diagnosis for both internal and external anatomy of the brain. (© **Medical Body Scans/ Photo Researchers, Inc.**)

confounding variables that may interfere with accurate assessment of the patient's ability to process information. Popular and long-standing neuropsychological assessment tools include the series of Wechsler Memory and Intelligence Scales, the Halstead-Reitan Neuropsychological Battery, the Boston Diagnostic and Aphasia Screening Test, the Wisconsin Card Sorting Test, and the Peabody Individual Achievement Tests.

It should be noted that although neuropsychological testing strives to provide accurate, reasonable, and understandable answers to the questions posed by the ordering physician regarding the function of an individual's brain, it is not truly an *objective* test like a CT scan. A CT scan gives results that cannot be consciously altered by the tester or by the individual being tested and is therefore, by definition, an objective test. The answers obtained during neuropsychological testing, in contrast, can be influenced by the patient's level of cooperation with the testing. Thus, it is considered *subjective*. For example, if a person just doesn't want to do the math section of one of the tests, she will score poorly in that area, but that does not necessarily mean that she has a brain injury affecting the areas of the brain most involved in performing basic math.

Personality Testing

Often, certain tests developed to evaluate an individual's personality are performed along with neuropsychological testing, and these may also look at specific psychological risks such as depression or thought disorder. The most commonly used personality assessment tool is the *Minnesota Multiphasic Personality Inventory, Revised (MMPI-R)*, which contains validity scales that help determine whether the results are likely to be a true representation of an individual's underlying personality or may be biased by purposeful exaggeration.

I find neuropsychological testing to be most helpful later in the rehabilitation process when a motivated patient wants to know whether she can successfully return to work or school. By understanding her residual strengths and remaining weaknesses, the patient is in a better position to set realistic goals. Often patients can learn to compensate for their weaknesses, with reasonable accommodations permitted by schools or employers. But the information gleaned from this kind of evaluation also prevents them from experiencing the disappointment and failure that can come from setting unrealistic goals, or trying to do too much too soon. Obviously, a person who can no longer speak intelligibly would not be expected to return to work as a telephone receptionist, but sometimes the mismatch between abilities and goals is not so clear-cut. One of my biggest concerns for every patient is to prevent failure and the demoralization that accompanies it. A good brain-injury specialist of any medical discipline should study the patient's family history very carefully, go over his or her symptoms in detail (especially in cases of mild traumatic brain injury), and look at psychosocial stressors that may complicate the problem. Such stressors might be tension at home, pressure at work or school, problems in a relationship, or the emotional stress of menopause. Technology and test evaluations are vital tools in diagnosing brain injury but cannot completely replace experience, expertise, and good judgment.

Disabilities and Long-Term Consequences Result from Traumatic Brain Injury

National Institute of Neurological Disorders and Stroke

The National Institute of Neurological Disorders and Stroke is a division of the National Institutes of Health tasked with reducing the burden of neurological disease, including traumatic brain injury (TBI). In the following selection, the authors describe the types of disabilities that often result from TBI, such as postconcussion syndrome—which has symptoms such as dizziness, headache, problems with sleeping, and depression—and posttraumatic amnesia, in which patients forget events that happened before the accident (retrograde) or after the accident (anterograde). Other problems that can result include difficulties with language and communication, cognitive problems such as confusion or poor planning, and emotional and behavioral problems. According to the authors, TBI also increases the likelihood of developing other serious neurological conditions years or decades after the initial trauma, such as Alzheimer's or Parkinson's disease.

SOURCE: "What Disabilities Can Result from a TBI?; Are There Other Long-Term Problems Associated with a TBI?," *Traumatic Brain Injury: Hope Through Research*. Washington, DC: National Institute of Neurological Disorders and Stroke, April 15, 2011.

Disabilities resulting from a TBI [traumatic brain injury] depend upon the severity of the injury, the location of the injury, and the age and general health of the patient. Some common disabilities include problems with cognition (thinking, memory, and reasoning), sensory processing (sight, hearing, touch, taste, and smell), communication (expression and understanding), and behavior or mental health (depression, anxiety, personality changes, aggression, acting out, and social inappropriateness).

Within days to weeks of the head injury approximately 40 percent of TBI patients develop a host of troubling symptoms collectively called *postconcussion syndrome (PCS)*. A patient need not have suffered a concussion or loss of consciousness to develop the syndrome and many patients with mild TBI suffer from PCS. Symptoms include headache, dizziness, vertigo (a sensation of spinning around or of objects spinning around the patient), memory problems, trouble concentrating, sleeping problems, restlessness, irritability, apathy, depression, and anxiety. These symptoms may last for a few weeks after the head injury. The syndrome is more prevalent in patients who had psychiatric symptoms, such as depression or anxiety, before the injury. Treatment for PCS may include medicines for pain and psychiatric conditions, and psychotherapy and occupational therapy to develop coping skills.

Cognitive Problems

Cognition is a term used to describe the processes of thinking, reasoning, problem solving, information processing, and memory. Most patients with severe TBI, if they recover consciousness, suffer from cognitive disabilities, including the loss of many higher level mental skills. The most common cognitive impairment among severely head-injured patients is memory loss, characterized by some loss of specific memories and the partial inability to form or store new ones. Some of these patients may experience *post-traumatic amnesia (PTA)*, either anterograde or retrograde. Anterograde PTA is impaired memory of events that happened after the TBI, while retrograde PTA is impaired memory of events that happened before the TBI.

A speech therapist works with a patient with aphasia, a difficulty with understanding and producing written and spoken language. (© Blair Seitz/Photo Researchers, Inc.)

Many patients with mild to moderate head injuries who experience cognitive deficits become easily confused or distracted and have problems with concentration and attention. They also have problems with higher level, so-called executive functions, such as planning, organizing, abstract reasoning, problem solving, and making judgments, which may make it difficult to resume pre-injury work-related activities. Recovery from cognitive deficits is greatest within the first 6 months after the injury and more gradual after that. Patients with moderate to severe TBI have more problems with cognitive deficits than patients with mild TBI, but a history of several mild TBIs may have an additive effect, causing cognitive deficits equal to a moderate or severe injury.

Sensory Problems

Many TBI patients have sensory problems, especially problems with vision. Patients may not be able to register what they are seeing or may be slow to recognize objects. Also, TBI patients often have difficulty with hand-eye coordination. Because of this, TBI patients may be prone to bumping into or dropping objects, or may seem generally unsteady. TBI patients may have difficulty driving a car, working complex machinery, or playing sports. Other sensory deficits may include problems with hearing, smell, taste, or touch. Some TBI patients develop tinnitus, a ringing or roaring in the ears. A person with damage to the part of the brain that processes taste or smell may develop a persistent bitter taste in the mouth or perceive a persistent noxious smell. Damage to the part of the brain that controls the sense of touch may cause a TBI patient to develop persistent skin tingling, itching, or pain. Although rare, these conditions are hard to treat.

Problems with Language and Communication

Language and communication problems are common disabilities in TBI patients. Some may experience *aphasia*, defined as difficulty with understanding and producing spoken and written language; others may have difficulty with the more subtle aspects of communication, such as body language and emotional, non-verbal signals.

In *non-fluent aphasia*, also called Broca's aphasia or motor aphasia, TBI patients often have trouble recalling words and speaking in complete sentences. They may speak in broken phrases and pause frequently. Most patients are aware of these deficits and may become extremely frustrated. Patients with *fluent aphasia*, also called Wernicke's aphasia or sensory aphasia, display little meaning in their speech, even though they speak in complete sentences and use correct grammar. Instead, they speak in flowing gibberish, drawing out their sentences with non-essential and invented words. Many patients with fluent aphasia are unaware that they make little sense and become angry with others for not understanding them. Patients with *global aphasia* have extensive damage to the portions of the brain responsible for language and often suffer severe communication disabilities.

TBI patients may have problems with spoken language if the part of the brain that controls speech muscles is damaged. In this disorder, called *dysarthria*, the patient can think of the appropriate language, but cannot easily speak the words because they are unable to use the muscles needed to form the words and produce the sounds. Speech is often slow, slurred, and garbled. Some may have problems with intonation or inflection, called *prosodic dysfunction*. An important aspect

> ## FAST FACT
>
> A 2011 study funded by the Department of Defense reported that veterans diagnosed with traumatic brain injury had more than twice as high a risk of developing dementia.

Test of Variables of Attention (TOVA) Scores of Persons with Mild Traumatic Brain Injury Compared to Normal Subjects and High Performers

In the Test of Variables of Attention, subjects are instructed to press a switch whenever they see a particular visual appear on a computer screen, and not to press if a different visual appears. The computer program assesses their performance in terms of attention, impulse control, reaction time, and distractibility.

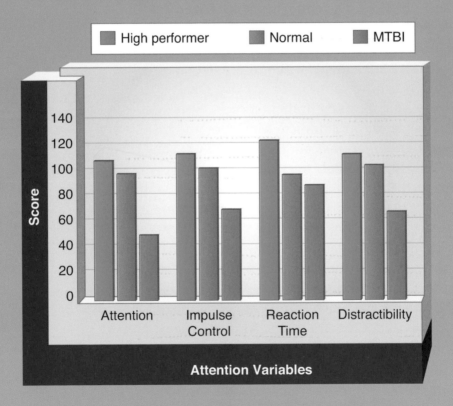

Taken from: "Post-Concussion Syndrome." Behavioral Neurotherapy Clinic, 2010.
www.adhd.com.au/Post_concussion_Syndrome.htm.

of speech, inflection conveys emotional meaning and is necessary for certain aspects of language, such as irony. These language deficits can lead to miscommunication, confusion, and frustration for the patient as well as those interacting with him or her.

Psychiatric Issues

Most TBI patients have emotional or behavioral problems that fit under the broad category of psychiatric health. Family members of TBI patients often find that personality changes and behavioral problems are the most difficult disabilities to handle. Psychiatric problems that may surface include depression, apathy, anxiety, irritability, anger, paranoia, confusion, frustration, agitation, insomnia or other sleep problems, and mood swings. Problem behaviors may include aggression and violence, impulsivity, disinhibition, acting out, noncompliance, social inappropriateness, emotional outbursts, childish behavior, impaired self-control, impaired self awareness, inability to take responsibility or accept criticism, egocentrism, inappropriate sexual activity, and alcohol or drug abuse/addiction. Some patients' personality problems may be so severe that they are diagnosed with borderline personality disorder, a psychiatric condition characterized by many of the problems mentioned above. Sometimes TBI patients suffer from developmental stagnation, meaning that they fail to mature emotionally, socially, or psychologically after the trauma. This is a serious problem for children and young adults who suffer from a TBI. Attitudes and behaviors that are appropriate for a child or teenager become inappropriate in adulthood. Many TBI patients who show psychiatric or behavioral problems can be helped with medication and psychotherapy.

Other Long-Term Problems

In addition to the immediate post-injury complications . . . , other long-term problems can develop after a TBI.

These include Parkinson's disease and other motor problems, Alzheimer's disease, *dementia pugilistica*, and post-traumatic dementia.

Alzheimer's disease (AD)—AD is a progressive, neurodegenerative disease characterized by dementia, memory loss, and deteriorating cognitive abilities. Recent research suggests an association between head injury in early adulthood and the development of AD later in life; the more severe the head injury, the greater the risk of developing AD. Some evidence indicates that a head injury may interact with other factors to trigger the disease and may hasten the onset of the disease in individuals already at risk. For example, people who have a particular form of the protein apolipoprotein E (apoE4) and suffer a head injury fall into this increased risk category. (ApoE4 is a naturally occurring protein that helps transport cholesterol through the bloodstream.)

Parkinson's disease and other motor problems—Movement disorders as a result of TBI are rare but can occur. Parkinson's disease may develop years after TBI as a result of damage to the basal ganglia. Symptoms of Parkinson's disease include tremor or trembling, rigidity or stiffness, slow movement (bradykinesia), inability to move (akinesia), shuffling walk, and stooped posture. . . . Other movement disorders that may develop after TBI include tremor, ataxia (uncoordinated muscle movements), and myoclonus (shock-like contractions of muscles).

Dementia pugilistica—Also called chronic traumatic encephalopathy, dementia pugilistica primarily affects career boxers. The most common symptoms of the condition are dementia and parkinsonism caused by repetitive blows to the head over a long period of time. Symptoms begin anywhere between 6 and 40 years after the start of a boxing career, with an average onset of about 16 years.

Post-traumatic dementia—The symptoms of post-traumatic dementia are very similar to those of dementia pugilistica, except that post-traumatic dementia is also characterized by long-term memory problems and is caused by a single, severe TBI that results in a coma.

Promising Research Benefits Future Brain Injury Treatments

National Institute of Neurological Disorders and Stroke

The National Institute of Neurological Disorders and Stroke (NINDS) is a division of the National Institutes of Health tasked with reducing the burden of neurological disease, including traumatic brain injury (TBI). In the following viewpoint, the author details research currently being conducted by NINDS into new ways of treating traumatic brain injury. According to the institute, after the initial brain trauma has occurred, a cascade of further damage to neurons (brain cells) results from damaged brain cells releasing excessive quantities of chemicals, which then damage or destroy nearby neurons. Promising research is being done into ways of blocking the secondary damage. In addition, research is being conducted into various ways of helping the brain to heal itself, for example by supporting the brain's natural *plasticity*, that is, its ability to adapt to injury and form new connections between neurons to replace those that were damaged.

SOURCE: National Institute of Neurological Disorders and Stroke, "What Research Is the NINDS Conducting?," Traumatic Brain Injury: Hope Through Research, April 15, 2011.

The National Institute of Neurological Disorders and Stroke (NINDS) conducts and supports research to better understand CNS [central nervous system] injury and the biological mechanisms underlying damage to the brain, to develop strategies and interventions to limit the primary and secondary brain damage that occurs within days of a head trauma, and to devise therapies to treat brain injury and help in long-term recovery of function.

On a microscopic scale, the brain is made up of billions of cells that interconnect and communicate.

The neuron is the main functional cell of the brain and nervous system, consisting of a cell body (soma), a tail or long nerve fiber (axon), and projections of the cell body called dendrites. The axons travel in tracts or clusters throughout the brain, providing extensive interconnections between brain areas.

One of the most pervasive types of injury following even a minor trauma is damage to the nerve cell's axon through shearing; this is referred to as diffuse axonal injury. This damage causes a series of reactions that eventually lead to swelling of the axon and disconnection from the cell body of the neuron. In addition, the part of the neuron that communicates with other neurons degenerates and releases toxic levels of chemical messengers called *neurotransmitters* into the synapse or space between neurons, damaging neighboring neurons through a secondary neuroexcitatory cascade. Therefore, neurons that were unharmed from the primary trauma suffer damage from this secondary insult. Many of these cells cannot survive the toxicity of the chemical onslaught and initiate programmed cell death, or *apoptosis*. This process usually takes place within the first 24 to 48 hours after the initial injury, but can be prolonged.

Protecting Brain Cells from Further Damage

One area of research that shows promise is the study of the role of calcium ion influx into the damaged neuron

Neural stem cells in a culture. Neural stem cells can be made into different types of nerve cells, or neurons.
(© Riccardo Cassiani-Ingoni/Photo Researchers, Inc.)

as a cause of cell death and general brain tissue swelling. Calcium enters nerve cells through damaged channels in the axon's membrane. The excess calcium inside the cell causes the axon to swell and also activates chemicals, called proteases, that break down proteins. One family of proteases, the calpains, are especially damaging to nerve cells because they break down proteins that maintain the structure of the axon. Excess calcium within the cell is also destructive to the cell's mitochondria, structures that produce the cell's energy. Mitochondria soak up excess calcium until they swell and stop functioning. If enough mitochondria are damaged, the nerve cell degenerates. Calcium influx has other damaging effects: it activates destructive enzymes, such as caspases that damage the DNA in the cell and trigger programmed cell death, and it damages sodium channels in the cell membrane, allowing sodium ions to flood the cell as well. Sodium influx exacerbates swelling of the cell body and axon.

NINDS researchers have shown, in both cell and animal studies, that giving specialized chemicals can reduce cell death caused by calcium ion influx. Other researchers have shown that the use of cyclosporin A, which blocks mitochondrial membrane permeability, protects axons from calcium influx. Another avenue of therapeutic intervention is the use of hypothermia (an induced state of low body temperature) to slow the progression of cell death and axon swelling.

In the healthy brain, the chemical glutamate functions as a neurotransmitter, but an excess amount of glutamate in the brain causes neurons to quickly overload from too much excitation, releasing toxic chemicals. These substances poison the chemical environment of surrounding cells, initiating degeneration and programmed cell death. Studies have shown that a group of enzymes called matrix metalloproteinases contribute to the toxicity by breaking down proteins that maintain the structure and order of the extracellular environment. Other research shows that glutamate reacts with calcium and sodium ion channels on the cell membrane, leading to an influx of calcium and sodium ions into the cell. Investigators are looking for ways to decrease the toxic effects of glutamate and other excitatory neurotransmitters.

Helping the Brain Repair Itself

The brain attempts to repair itself after a trauma, and is more successful after mild to moderate injury than after severe injury. Scientists have shown that after diffuse axonal injury neurons can spontaneously adapt and recover by sprouting some of the remaining healthy fibers of the neuron into the spaces once occupied by the degenerated axon. These fibers can develop in such a way that the neuron can resume communication with neighboring neurons. This is a very delicate process and can be disrupted by any of a number of factors, such as *neuro-excitation*, hypoxia (low oxygen levels), and hypotension (low blood flow). Following trauma, excessive neuroexcitation, that is the electrical activation of nerve cells or fibers, especially disrupts this natural recovery process and can cause sprouting fibers to lose direction and connect with the wrong terminals.

Scientists suspect that these misconnections may contribute to some long-term disabilities, such as pain, spasticity, seizures, and memory problems. NINDS researchers are trying to learn more about the brain's natural recovery process and what factors or triggers control it. They hope that through manipulation of these triggers they can increase repair while decreasing misconnections.

NINDS investigators are also looking at larger, tissue-specific changes within the brain after a TBI [traumatic brain injury], Researchers have shown that trauma to the frontal lobes of the brain can damage specific chemical messenger systems, specifically the dopaminergic system, the collection of neurons in the brain that uses the neurotransmitter dopamine. Dopamine is an important chemical messenger—for example, degeneration of dopamine-producing neurons is the primary cause of Parkinson's disease. NINDS researchers are studying how the dopaminergic system responds after a TBI and its relationship to neurodegeneration and Parkinson's disease.

Stem Cells and Plasticity

The use of stem cells to repair or replace damaged brain tissue is a new and exciting avenue of research. A *neural stem cell* is a special kind of cell that can multiply and give rise to other more specialized cell types. These cells are found in adult neural tissue and normally develop into several different cell types found within the central nervous system. NINDS researchers are investigating the ability of stem cells to develop into neurotransmitter-producing neurons, specifically dopamine-producing cells. Researchers are also looking at the power of stem cells to develop into *oligodendrocytes*, a type of brain cell that produces myelin, the fatty sheath that surrounds and insulates axons. One study in mice has shown that bone marrow stem cells can develop into neurons, demonstrating that neural stem cells are not the only type of stem cell that could be beneficial in the treatment of brain and nervous system disorders. At the moment, stem cell research for TBI is in its infancy, but future research may lead to advances for treatment and rehabilitation.

In addition to the basic research described above, NINDS scientists also conduct broader based clinical research involving patients. One area of study focuses on the *plasticity* of the brain after injury. In the strictest sense, plasticity means the ability to be formed or molded. When speaking of the brain, plasticity means the ability of the brain to adapt to deficits and injury. NINDS researchers are investigating the extent of brain plasticity after injury and developing therapies to enhance plasticity as a means of restoring function.

> **FAST FACT**
>
> A 2007 University of California study found that brain-injured mice showed enhanced memory (similar to healthy mice) for up to three months after being treated with stem cells.

The plasticity of the brain and the rewiring of neural connections make it possible for one part of the brain to take up the functions of a disabled part. Scientists have long known that the immature brain is generally more plastic than the mature brain, and that the brains of children are better able to adapt and recover from injury than the brains of adults. NINDS researchers are investigating the mechanisms underlying this difference and theorize that children have an overabundance of hard-wired neural networks, many of which naturally decrease through a process called *pruning*. When an injury destroys an important neural network in children, another less useful neural network that would have eventually died takes over the responsibilities of the damaged network. Some researchers are looking at the role of plasticity in memory, while others are using imaging

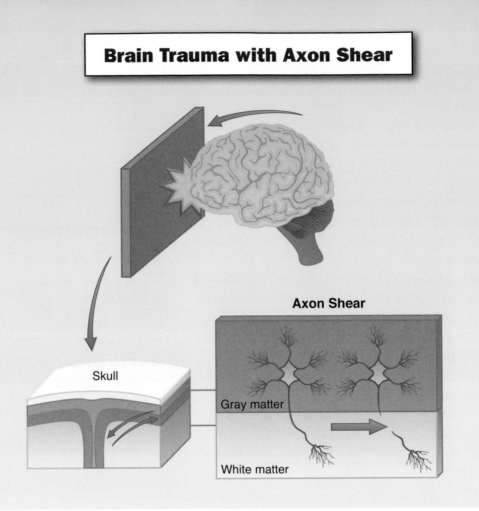

Brain Trauma with Axon Shear

Axon Shear

Skull

Gray matter

White matter

technologies, such as functional MRI, to map regions of the brain and record evidence of plasticity.

Another important area of research involves the development of improved rehabilitation programs for those who have disabilities from a TBI. The Congressional Children's Health Act of 2000 authorized the NINDS to conduct and support research related to TBI with the goal of designing therapies to restore normal functioning in cognition and behavior.

Clinical Trials Research

The NINDS works to develop treatments that can be given in the first hours after a TBI, hoping that quick action can prevent or reverse much of the brain damage resulting from the injury. A recently completed NINDS-supported clinical trial involved lowering body temperature in TBI patients to 33 degrees Celsius within 8 hours of the trauma. Although the investigators found that the treatment did not improve outcome overall, they did learn that patients younger than 45 years who were admitted to the hospital already in a hypothermic state fared better if they were kept cool than if they were brought to normal body temperature. Other ongoing clinical trials include the use of hypothermia for severe TBI in children, the use of magnesium sulfate to protect nerve cells after TBI, and the effects of lowering ICP [intracranial pressure] and increasing cerebral blood flow.

CHAPTER 2

Controversies Concerning Traumatic Brain Injury

Progress Is Being Made in Helping Soldiers with Traumatic Brain Injury

Michael S. Jaffee

Michael S. Jaffee is the national director of the Defense and Veterans Brain Injury Center (DVBIC), a congressionally mandated collaboration between the Department of Defense (DOD) and the Department of Veterans Affairs (VA). In the following viewpoint, Jaffee asserts that the DVBIC is proactive in treating soldiers who suffer from traumatic brain injury (TBI). He details many steps that have been taken to prevent TBI when possible, and to ensure that soldiers with brain injuries are accurately diagnosed and treated promptly and comprehensively. According to Jaffee, prevention is accomplished through the use of personal protective equipment and education of soldiers in risk mitigation. He says that special screening tests have been developed to aid early detection, for example, the Military Acute Concussion Evaluation test, which is administered in the war zone following an incident. Extensive treatment and rehabilitation programs have also been put in place, Jaffee claims, and research into future treatments is being promoted.

Photo on facing page. There has been renewed concern about head injuries in youth sports. (© Mark Clarke/ Photo Researchers, Inc.)

SOURCE: Michael S. Jaffee, Prepared Statement, *Progress in Treating the Signature Wounds of the Current Conflicts,* Hearing Before the Committee on Veterans' Affairs United States Senate, 111th Congress, 1st session, US Government Printing Office, May 5, 2010.

I am honored to be able to represent DOD [Department of Defense], and the men and women who serve in our Military Health System. I am the National Director of the Defense and Veterans Brain Injury Center (DVBIC), a congressionally mandated collaboration between DOD and VA [Department of Veterans Affairs] which is organized as a network of excellence across 17 DOD and VA sites with more than 225 professionals representing more than 20 different clinical disciplines. For the past two and a half years, the DVBIC has also operated as the primary operational TBI [traumatic brain injury] center of DCoE [Defense Centers of Excellence for Psychological Health and Traumatic Brain Injury]. Through these collaborations, I have been fortunate to work closely and collaboratively with our colleagues across DOD and VA for the last several years. I am proud of what we have accomplished together to advance the prevention, diagnosis, and treatment of Servicemembers and veterans with TBI. I am confident in our organization's ability to serve as a national asset for helping Servicemembers and veterans maximize their functional abilities and decrease or eliminate their TBI-related disabilities.

The high rate of TBI and blast-related concussion events resulting from current combat operations directly impacts the health and safety of individual Servicemembers and subsequently the level of unit readiness and troop retention. The impacts of TBI are felt within each branch of the Service and throughout both the DOD and VA health care systems. Since January 2003, over 134,000 Servicemembers have been identified within our surveillance system as having sustained a clinician-confirmed TBI, most of which are considered mild TBI or a concussion (mTBI). It is important to note almost 90 percent of individuals who sustain mTBI will have complete resolution of their symptoms within days or weeks of the incident. Our in-theater management guidelines for TBI emphasize safety and prevention of recurrent injuries until recovery has occurred.

With the support of Congress, both Departments have dedicated significant resources to the prevention, early detection, treatment, and rehabilitation of Servicemembers and veterans with TBI. Ongoing medical research continues to contribute to our understanding of each of these activities. I will describe our efforts in these areas. . . .

Prevention

Prevention of TBI is a critical component of our overall strategy. Central to the preventative approach is the continued development of state-of-the-art personal protective equipment (PPE). The army combat helmet/light weight helmet was developed for today's battlefield environment, and a next generation enhanced combat helmet is under development. The Headborne System—a joint Service future initiative—is being engineered to provide added protection from blast injury.

Along with PPE investments, the Department has engaged in a broad-based awareness campaign to provide Servicemembers with strategies to mitigate risks both in a deployed location and at home to include ballistics protection and adherence to use of seatbelts.

Early Detection

Our early detection efforts are focused on identifying potential TBI as close to the time of injury as possible. Mandatory concussion screening occurs at four levels to maximize treatment opportunities for Servicemembers who may have sustained a concussion: in-theater; at Landstuhl Regional Medical Center, Germany (for all medically evacuated personnel); during Post Deployment Health Assessments and Reassessments; and at VA facilities when veterans are treated.

DOD has developed and proliferated—with the input of the Services, VA, and civilian subject matter experts—a systematic method for conducting these screenings with

Evacuation and Treatment of Soldiers with Traumatic Brain Injury

Patients with traumatic brain injuries in war zones are rapidly transported through specialized centers in the army's sophisticated modern trauma system.

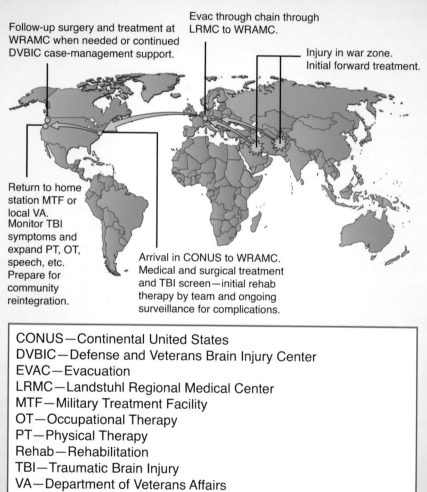

Follow-up surgery and treatment at WRAMC when needed or continued DVBIC case-management support.

Evac through chain through LRMC to WRAMC.

Injury in war zone. Initial forward treatment.

Return to home station MTF or local VA. Monitor TBI symptoms and expand PT, OT, speech, etc. Prepare for community reintegration.

Arrival in CONUS to WRAMC. Medical and surgical treatment and TBI screen—initial rehab therapy by team and ongoing surveillance for complications.

CONUS—Continental United States
DVBIC—Defense and Veterans Brain Injury Center
EVAC—Evacuation
LRMC—Landstuhl Regional Medical Center
MTF—Military Treatment Facility
OT—Occupational Therapy
PT—Physical Therapy
Rehab—Rehabilitation
TBI—Traumatic Brain Injury
VA—Department of Veterans Affairs
WRAMC—Walter Reed Army Medical Center

Taken from: Michael S. Jaffee, et. al. "Acute Clinical Care and Care Coordination for Traumatic Brain Injury within Department of Defense." *JRRD*, 2009.

the appropriate tools. The Military Acute Concussion Evaluation (MACE) has been used for in-theater screening following an incident. This evaluation tool has been independently reviewed by the Institute of Medicine and recommended for continued use in assessing combat-related TBI. We continue a cycle of process improvement for in-theater screening and management. The latest proposed guidelines include a transition to mandatory evaluation of all Servicemembers involved in an incident considered associated with risk of concussion. DOD and VA jointly developed and are using a screening tool in the Post-Deployment Health Assessment and Re-assessment and the VA TBI Clinical Reminder. This tool is an adaptation of the Brief TBI Screen and has been recommended to DOD by the Institute of Medicine for this purpose.

Treatment

DOD has published clinical practice guidelines for both in-theater and CONUS [continental United States]–based management of mTBI ("Mild TBI Clinical Guidelines in the Deployed Setting" and "Mild TBI Clinical Guidance"), and developed tailored algorithms for use by medics/corpsmen, an initial evaluation, and a more comprehensive evaluation. NATO [North Atlantic Treaty Organization] countries have used adaptations of the MACE and DOD clinical guidelines as a template for their own militaries.

For providers delivering care in the combat theater, we have introduced an electronic consult service for use by all Service providers to connect them with a TBI expert—jointly manned by DOD and VA specialists. This consult service has proven to be a useful tool to deployed medical staffs.

DOD and VA worked closely on developing and issuing evidence-based CONUS guidelines for management of mTBI. We issued these guidelines in April 2009, to providers in both organizations, assisting them with patients having subacute or chronic (more than 90 days) mTBI. These guidelines allow Servicemembers to receive care from their primary care providers, closest to home and family support. When required, referrals are made to TBI specialists at designated facilities.

For more severe categories of TBI, we have disseminated several guidelines for use in theater, and have sponsored the development of specialist guidelines such as those from the American Association of Neuroscience Nurses. We have also provided consultation in the development of civilian guidelines such as those developed by the American College of Emergency Physicians.

FAST FACT

Patients at the Department of Veterans Affairs "emerging consciousness" treatment facilities are recovering from coma at a rate of nearly 70 percent, according to a 2010 report in *USA Today*.

To advance our understanding of changes in neurocognitive abilities, we have implemented a program of baseline, pre-deployment cognitive evaluation. Introduced in 2008, this baseline test better informs return-to-duty determinations in theater following a concussion injury.

The DVBIC also facilitated a consensus conference on programs for minimally conscious TBI patients which included DOD, VA, and civilian subject matter experts. This conference was instrumental in helping inform further development of relevant programs to manage this population.

Finally, our clinical guidelines recognize there are often co-morbidities with TBI cases, to include depression, post-traumatic stress and substance use disorders, and other extremity injuries. To better understand this, the DVBIC co-sponsored with the Congressional Brain Injury Task Force, an international symposium on behavioral health and TBI. TBI case management demands an interdisciplinary endeavor that must incorporate and meld various clinical elements including neurology, neurosurgery, psychiatry, neuropsychology, and physical medicine and rehabilitation. DOD and VA have worked to ensure our TBI clinical guidelines represent the input from this diverse set of medical specialists.

An independent article published by the *Journal of Head Trauma Rehabilitation* cited the DVBIC collaboration between DOD and VA as the most fully developed system of care in the United States for brain injury.

Rehabilitation/Recovery/Reintegration

Rehabilitation is an essential component of our TBI program, with a focused approach on cognitive rehabilitation. In 2009, we hosted the leading experts in this country—from DOD, VA, and the civilian sector—to develop and issue clinical guidance for cognitive rehabilitation programs based on available evidence. Fourteen DOD military treatment facilities will use these guidelines in a controlled, step-wise process to assess the effectiveness of these guidelines on patient outcomes.

The US Army has been using new therapies to treat brain injuries. Here, a soldier uses a driving simulator to test reaction skills for treatment of a traumatic brain injury. (© AP Images/Lolita Baldor)

The DVBIC has worked with VA on the Assisted Living for Veterans with TBI project. We have collaborated with VA in their exploration of means to contract with civilian facilities to serve veterans. We helped establish a pilot age-appropriate TBI-specific assisted living program with multidisciplinary rehabilitation and assistive technology at one of nine state-owned comprehensive rehabilitation facilities. . . .

Ongoing Research

The short- and long-term effects of blast injury on the brain are still not completely known. DOD has made important contributions to the medical literature with our own research, to include a history of published, successful randomized-controlled clinical trials and several awards from national professional organizations.

The Medical Research and Materiel Command and DVBIC convened a consensus conference with 75 experts identifying scientific evidence supporting the importance of blast injury. Last year [2009], DVBIC published the largest randomized controlled trial of cognitive rehabilitation for moderate-severe patients. The Department's TBI research contributions were recognized in the external technical report on mTBI in DOD conducted by the Survivability/Vulnerability Information Analysis Center which stated in its conclusion:

> Even within the limited existing literature, it is evident that researchers are now making use of screening criteria, instruments, and other resources developed and made available through DVBIC. The DVBIC now plays a central role in performing and advancing research that will directly benefit military Servicemembers and veterans with TBI.

With the support of Congress, DOD is leveraging national expertise and resources in TBI research through the Congressionally Directed Medical Research Program by investing more than $200 million to academic researchers after a process of scientific and programmatic review that included our VA colleagues.

We are working on innovative ways to enhance our system to fast-track promising research initiatives and findings, and rapidly identify gaps such as the paucity of research findings regarding clinical outcomes from cognitive rehabilitation in the concussion population, as well as direct resources to address these gaps.

DOD and VA are collaborating further with other Federal agencies on translational biophysics, proteomics, and other blast-related projects.

Soldiers with Traumatic Brain Injury Are Not Getting the Help They Need

Sarah Wade

Sarah Wade is a coordinator for family issues and traumatic brain injury for the Wounded Warriors Project. Her husband, Ted, has a severe traumatic brain injury (TBI) received while serving in the Iraq war in 2004. In the following viewpoint, Wade argues that the Department of Veterans Affairs (VA) is not giving veterans with TBI the medical care they require. Wade claims that individualized treatment plans, while required by law, are often not provided to caregivers or are not done properly. She contends the VA is not able to handle the full range of treatments that may be needed by each case of TBI yet is frequently resistant to bringing in outside help when needed. According to Wade, another significant gap is that the VA will not provide nonmedical support such as life-skills coaching, supported employment, or community-reintegration therapy, even though those types of treatment are needed for a soldier with a TBI to make a full recovery.

SOURCE: Sarah Wade, Prepared Statement, *Progress in Treating the Signature Wounds of the Current Conflicts,* Hearing Before the Committee on Veterans' Affairs United States Senate, 111th Congress, 1st session, US Government Printing Office, May 5, 2010.

Each case of Traumatic Brain Injury [TBI] is unique. Depending on the site of the injury and other factors, patients may experience a wide range of medical and related physical effects—from profound neurological deficits, to problems with speaking, vision, eating, incontinence, etc.—as well as dramatic behavioral symptoms and cognitive deficits. As VA [Department of Veterans Affairs] clinicians themselves recognize, it is difficult to predict a person's ultimate level of recovery. But to be effective in helping an individual recover from a brain injury and return to a life as independent and productive as possible, rehabilitation must be targeted to the specific needs of the individual patient. In VA parlance, rehabilitation must be "veteran-centered." This simple principle is a critical touchstone by which to gauge VA's progress in TBI care. Is VA providing "veteran-centered TBI care?" We see progress; but the system does not live up to the VA's claim of "world class" service, in our view. Let me highlight some of the critical gaps.

Access to the Right Services

Given that every case of TBI is unique and each patient's care and rehabilitative needs differ, it is unrealistic to believe that every VA medical center, or even most, can have the needed range of expertise "in-house" to meet the wide-ranging, often complex needs of all TBI patients. WWP's [Wounded Warrior Project's] experience is that even the over 100 VA facilities that have received additional staffing, equipment and training and constitute its TBI/Polytrauma System of Care are not fully equipped to provide the wide range of services TBI patients need.

Even a facility with the most well-equipped, well-staffed rehabilitation service may not be the right setting for some TBI patients. A young veteran who needs help with community reintegration and relearning basic life skills cannot be expected to make meaningful gains in a geriatric facility. Too often, VA TBI care for OEF/OIF

[Operation Enduring Freedom (Afghanistan)/Operation Iraqi Freedom (Iraq)] veterans is not age-appropriate.

Unlike the Army's willingness to bring in outside experts when it was not fully prepared to meet [my husband] Ted's clinical needs, my own experience and that of other families is that VA facilities have been much less open to acknowledge limitations in expertise or lack of options when they exist and to offer alternatives that might produce better outcomes. . . . With greater congressional focus on the issue, VA has demonstrated greater openness to authorizing non-VA sources to provide rehab services that are not available at, or cannot feasibly be provided, through VA facilities. But surely in a veteran-centered system of care a patient's spouse would not have to take the lead on researching how best to meet her husband's rehabilitative needs and have to press to get those services approved. And . . . a more veteran-centered system would not so routinely reject such requests.

Individualized Rehabilitation Plans

VA has . . . [stated] that "[a]n individualized rehabilitation and community reintegration plan is developed for every Veteran and active duty Service member who requires ongoing rehabilitation care for TBI;" VA has also reported . . . that "[t]he patient and family participate in development of the treatment plan and receive a copy of the plan from the care coordinator." Of course, VA is required by law to develop such plans, engage family and veteran in the plan's development, and provide copies of the plan to the veteran and family. But caregivers with whom I've worked closely have never seen a rehabilitation plan, and—while they acknowledge that VA clinicians may develop a plan— they report that they have not been afforded an opportunity to play a role in its development. I have seen a VA document that was described to me as a veteran's TBI rehab plan but was little more than a list of the services VA would be providing or had authorized. In contrast, the law

makes it clear that these plans are to include rehabilitative objectives for improving the physical, cognitive, and vocational functioning of the individual with the goal of maximizing the independence and reintegration of such individual into the community. It is critical, in our view, that those rehab objectives are clearly identified, and that the veteran and family are active participants in setting those objectives and in identifying the specific treatments and services to be provided to achieve those objectives. Effective rehabilitation requires that providers, patients and their families work together to achieve the best possible outcomes. That must start with rehabilitation planning. Veteran-centered rehabilitation demands no less.

Sarah Wade, the viewpoint author, testifies before the President's Commission on Care for America's Returning Wounded Warriors about her struggles caring for her husband, who suffered a traumatic brain injury in Iraq. (© **AP Images/ Charles Dharapak**)

Effectiveness of Case-Management and Care-Coordination

The Federal Recovery Coordination Program has proven an exceptional initiative in assisting many who were severely injured in Iraq and Afghanistan, and their families, to access needed care, services, and benefits. It has been especially important for veterans with multiple complex needs, such as those with severe TBI. But as the program was not established until 2007, many who were severely wounded earlier in the war and who are still struggling years after their injuries, lack this singular support. In all, only about 460 warriors have Federal Recovery Coordinators (FRC's). There is a clear need to augment the number of FRC's assigned to help wounded warriors, particularly those with the complex needs associated with a severe brain injury.

But as helpful as FRCs have been in removing barriers to services, having an FRC does not solve all problems. Not all case-managers and care-coordinators necessarily have experience with brain injury. And as FRC's are for the most part located at a handful of key DOD [Department of Defense] acute-care facilities, these individuals are generally not familiar with the resources in the veteran's community. Given deep resistance at many VA facilities to draw on community expertise, the FRC's limited ability to navigate locally is concerning. But an even more fundamental, troubling issue is the deeply engrained culture of "no" that too often confronts veterans and their advocates, whether parents, spouses, or care-coordinators attempting to meet the veteran's needs. Too often, VA facilities do not seem hesitant to say "no" to FRCs. In short, the individual case-management assistance afforded by an FRC is no substitute for more thorough-going system changes.

Scope and Duration of Rehabilitative Services

While many VA facilities have dedicated rehabilitation physicians, therapists and other specialists, the scope of services actually provided these veterans is often limited, both in duration and in the range of services VA will provide or authorize. Such barriers needlessly constrain rehabilitative and long-term care options, and as a result, prevent too many veterans with severe TBI from attaining their goal of continued recovery and maximum quality of life.

The literature indicates that some people make a good recovery after suffering a severe TBI. But many have considerable difficulty with community integration even after undergoing rehabilitative care, and may need further services and supports. But it is all too common for families—reliant on VA to help a loved one recover after sustaining a severe Traumatic Brain Injury—to be told that VA can no longer provide a particular service because the veteran is no longer making significant progress. Imagine the frustration and feeling of abandonment when a Department whose mission is to "care for him who has borne the battle" says, "no more therapy!"

It is not clear whether VA's failure to provide veterans who sustained severe TBI with ongoing maintenance rehabilitation is based on a perception that VA's statutory authority is limited to therapy to "regain function," on cost concerns, or on other consideration. But it is clear that ongoing rehabilitation is often needed to maintain function. Whatever the explanation for limiting the duration of a veteran's therapy, there is profound reason for concern that many veterans denied maintenance therapy will regress, losing cognitive, physical and other gains made during earlier rehabilitation.

Significantly, VA facilities are also denying requests to provide TBI patients with what might be deemed "non-medical" supports. Yet supports like community-reintegration therapy, life-skills coaching, or supported employment, for example, afford the veteran the opportunity to gain greater independence and improved quality of life. Given TBI sequellae [pathological conditions resulting from the brain injury] that cause individuals considerable difficulty re-integrating into the community, VA's

> **FAST FACT**
>
> In 2008 a Rand Corporation report estimated that 320,000 US soldiers in Iraq and Afghanistan had suffered traumatic brain injuries, out of the 1.64 million serving in those countries.

How Explosions Cause Traumatic Brain Injuries in Soldiers

Primary Blast Injury

An explosion generates a blast wave traveling faster than sound and creating a surge of high pressure followed by a vacuum. Studies show that the blast wave shoots through armor and soldiers' skulls and brains, even if it does not draw blood. While the exact mechanisms by which it damages the brain's cells and circuits are still being studied, the blast wave's pressure has been shown to compress the torso, impacting blood vessels, which send damaging energy pulses into the brain. The pressure can also be transferred partially through the skull, interacting with the brain.

Blast wave

Energy Pulse

Secondary Blast Injury

Shrapnel and debris propelled by the blast can strike a soldier's head, causing either a closed-head injury through blunt force or a penetrating head injury that damages brain tissue.

Shrapnel

Tertiary Blast Injury

The kinetic energy generated and released by an explosion can accelerate a soldier's body through the air and into the ground or nearby solid object. Once the body stops, the brain continues to move in one direction of the force, hitting the interior of the skull and then bouncing back into the opposite side, causing a coup-contrecoup injury.

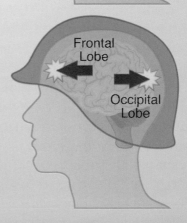

Frontal Lobe

Occipital Lobe

Taken from: Christian Miller, Daniel Zwerdling, Susanne Reber, and Robin Fields. "Brain Wars: How the Military Is Failing Its Wounded." Dart Center for Journalism & Trauma, April 14th, 2011. http://dartcenter.org.

rigid adherence to a medical model of rehabilitation—and foreclosing social supports—is a formula for denying a veteran the promise of full recovery. . . .

Veteran-Centered Care

VA leaders have taken important steps toward establishing both a TBI system of care and policies aimed at fostering optimal recoveries for veterans and service members with severe TBI. But deep, troubling gaps in that system are compromising realization of too many veterans' potential for full rehabilitation. This must change—and the needed change must be in a single direction—toward truly veteran-centered care.

The principle of veteran-centered care must be more than a slogan. It must be a core value at the heart of VA's TBI program. If rehabilitation and care is to be veteran-centered, VA facilities must develop truly individualized rehabilitation plans built around goals developed in concert with the veteran and his/her family. Those plans must also provide for access to all "appropriate rehabilitative components," a requirement that encompasses "age-appropriate" services. Providing veteran-centered care also requires a fundamental change aimed at meeting each veteran's rehabilitation needs—whether through services VA provides or procures. If VA TBI care is to be veteran-centered and "world class," it can no longer reflect an approach that says, in effect, "we don't provide that service; you'll have to accept our service or pay for the care you want out of pocket." Successful rehabilitation must build on the strengths and needs of the injured individual; requiring the injured veteran to adapt to arbitrary VA requirements or limitations is a sure path to rehabilitative failure. To put it another way, VA must become a system that looks for ways to say "yes," rather than "no."

Concussions in Youth Sports Need to Be Taken More Seriously

Sean Fine

Sean Fine is an editorial writer for the Ontario, Canada, newspaper the *Globe and Mail.* In the following viewpoint, Fine argues that the health consequences of sports-related concussions in young athletes is being downplayed by parents, coaches, and the players themselves. Fine gives examples of parents and coaches allowing young athletes to continue playing despite concussions and refers to a study in which qualified physicians observing hockey games found a much higher rate of concussion than was being reported. According to Fine, brain damage from concussions is cumulative, so the risk of additional concussions needs to be taken particularly seriously. He references the case of Sidney Crosby, a professional hockey player who suffered two concussions in one week, resulting in serious, lingering health consequences. The author also discusses his thirteen-year-old daughter, an enthusiastic athlete who has had a concussion yet is determined to continue playing multiple sports.

My daughter flew toward the ball, her neck outstretched, as graceful and ferocious as a Canada goose. Someone else's daughter hurtled, gooselike, toward her. A sickening craaaccck as skull met skull.

I suppose Claire was lucky. Within a few minutes, her face and forehead wore a blazing imprint of the other girl's head. She complained that she could not see out of one eye. "The referee looks like Voldemort."

Yes, lucky. It was as if her concussion on the soccer field that day was made visible. We had sat on the bench together, waiting to see how she felt. Now, it was impossible to deny, minimize, ignore. Impossible to put her back out on the field that day. (It would be hard to call the other girl lucky. Her nose was broken, and she was taken to the hospital.)

Claire is tough. A 13-year-old girl, blond and beautiful, and as unwilling as any pro athlete—Sidney Crosby [a Canadian hockey player], to name one—to take herself out of a game. Yup, I'm a little proud. Maybe just proud enough to be stupid with her health, under different circumstances.

Risk my daughter's brain, for a game? Would any capable parent do such a thing?

They do. All the time. In a study led by sports doctor Paul Echlin of London, [Ontario,] independent physicians and neutral observers monitored two junior hockey teams with players 16 to 21 years old. During the 52 games they observed at rinkside, they diagnosed 21 concussions. That is seven times the highest rate ever recorded for hockey.

Those physicians found concussions because they looked for them, and because they knew what to look for. And yet a coach, a team executive and even several parents balked at keeping concussed players out of the lineup. And this was a fourth-tier league.

"During the playoffs," Dr. Echlin writes, "Coach B's son suffered an apparent third concussion of the season.

. . . Nevertheless, Coach B's son was permitted to play the rest of the game without the suggested medical evaluation."

I'm no Coach B, no crazed stage parent, but what did I know about concussions? I'm a little bit haunted by what might have happened. Would I have let Claire return to the game if (like Sidney Crosby, mashed in the head last month [January 2011] at the Winter Classic in Pittsburgh, Pennsylvania) there had been no giant welt and no Voldemort? And what if I hadn't been there that day? Would she now be brain-injured like Sidney?

Concussion Damage Is Cumulative

Claire's head hurt. We drove—interminably— from the exurban tournament to a city hospital. In the emergency ward, a drug addict seated next to Claire threw up. We switched seats, cuddled and talked about the [Toronto] Blue Jays' [American League] pennant chances.

At last, a doctor was available. No CT [computed tomography] scan, she said. The radiation can damage the growing brain. Claire's sore eye appeared to be fine. The doctor handed me a sheet from ThinkFirst, neurosurgeon Charles Tator's group, setting out the stages a concussed athlete needs to go through before returning to play.

The first concussion isn't usually a big worry, she said. "It's the second one you need to worry about. The damage is cumulative."

And Claire wanted to play again. Not just soccer. Everything.

Hockey season was about to begin. And football tryouts at her middle school. (There's a girls' touch football team.) And, three weeks away, practices for the fall-winter indoor soccer season.

She's an athlete. An athlete plays until the final bell. To ask, "Are you okay, do you want to go back in," is

FAST FACT

Time magazine reports that between 2005 and 2008, 41 percent of high school athletes with concussions returned to play sooner than suggested by American Academy of Neurology guidelines.

Percentage Who Would Play a Concussed Star

Percent of those asked in an *ESPN The Magazine* poll in November 2010, "Your team is in the state title game, and your star gets a concussion. Would you rather lose the game as he sits out, or win it because he chose to play with it?"

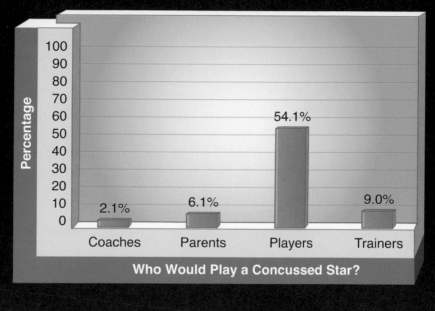

Taken from: Hans Gissinger. "Concussion Confidential." *ESPN The Magazine*, Dec. 19, 2010. http://sports.espn.go.com.

to place the burden of choice on the wrong shoulders. If Sidney Crosby could be so wrong about returning to play, what is the likelihood Claire would make the right decision for herself?

No parent should leave that choice to the child. In what other important sphere are children or teens routinely permitted that autonomy? Would you like to stay out until midnight, Claire? Get together with someone you met over the Internet?

I tried to talk to her about the damage done by repeated concussions. Her rebuttals were unyielding and uninformed. (And she wants to be a doctor!) It should not be a young person's job to safeguard her own brain health. It's the parent's.

Historical Perspectives

Am I being a wimp? In William Wellman's classic film *The Happy Years*, set in 1896, prep-school boys play tackle football without equipment. A wedge of blockers steamrolls the diminutive hero. He's unconscious briefly, but his teammates drag him to his feet and he crouches for the next play. People were tough in those days, I thought. It didn't hurt anyone. But then I remembered—people died all the time in football back then. Those flying masses of wedges were homicidal. In 1905, 18 people were killed playing football in the United States. President Theodore Roosevelt demanded something be done, and the game changed.

It feels a bit like 1896 to me. Two years ago, the brain of a dead hockey player, Reggie Fleming, was scanned

Pittsburgh Penguins star Sidney Crosby became the poster boy for concussions when he received two concussions in one week that kept him from playing hockey for a year. (© AP Images/Gene J. Puskar)

and showed signs of chronic traumatic encephalopathy, a degenerative disease that leads to dementia. In football, players at the University of North Carolina receive an average of 950 hits to the head in a season of games and practices. What lifelong traumas are we setting up our best and bravest athletes for? Even some teenage athletes are suffering cognitive problems or sensitivity to light and sound.

I took my daughter to her pediatrician to ask for a medical clearance before she returned to play. Yes, she could return, no problem at all, the doctor said. On the other hand, a second concussion would be bad. Is that a conundrum or a paradox? Whatever it is, it was difficult to square. In the end, I decided to limit Claire to two sports at a time. Soccer would have to wait until football season was over.

I have a neighbour who played professional hockey in Europe. You'd have a fight, he said, be knocked out, and come back for the next period. He laughed about it. It hadn't hurt him. Hahaha. I know a coach of the local learn-to-play hockey program whose grown son suffered eight concussions in youth hockey. "The doctor said one more and he could be a vegetable," the coach told me. Hahaha.

My daughter is playing soccer again. One day last month, her teammate aimed a corner kick for the front of the net, and once again Claire flew through the air, neck outstretched like a goose . . . the goalie rushed out . . . Claire's head struck the ball, artfully, beautifully, and she scored, and the other parents cheered wildly.

I did too.

Children with Traumatic Brain Injuries Are Not Getting the Long-Term Help They Need

Marilyn Lash

Marilyn Lash has a master's in social work and is president and senior editor of Lash and Associates Publishing/Training Inc. In the following viewpoint, Lash argues that children who have suffered traumatic brain injury (TBI) are not getting the help with recovery and rehabilitation that they need. She says that because children often heal from their physical injuries quickly, it is falsely believed that their overall recovery will continue to be rapid and that they will recover completely; however, as brain development proceeds, new deficits may be revealed as damaged brain areas are newly challenged in the school system. Despite this, Lash asserts that rehabilitation services are much less available for children than for adults. For example, she notes that fewer than 2 percent of children and teens with TBI receive special education services.

SOURCE: Marilyn Lash, "Child's Recovery After Traumatic Brain Injury Takes Time," *Blog on Brain Injury,* Lash & Associates Publishing/ Training, Inc., May 24, 2010. www.lapublishing.com. © 2010 by Lash and Associates Publishing/Training, Inc. All rights reserved. Reproduced by permission.

Traumatic brain injury in childhood is the most prevalent cause of death and long-term disability in children and affects all socioeconomic levels [according to Sandra Chapman in a 2006 article in *Brain Injury/Professional*]. The recovery process for children is more complex than for adults because the child's brain is still developing. Certainly, the severity of the injury to the brain affects outcome, but other factors are also critical including the child's age when injured and secondary brain damage due to brain swelling. The delivery of emergency medical services directly impacts survival rates as does the provision of expert trauma care.

For a long time, it was believed that children were more resilient than adults after a traumatic brain injury (TBI). It is now understood that the rapid physical recovery often seen in children with TBI can be misleading. As the child emerges from coma and progresses with physical, occupational and speech/language therapies, parents often speak of a "miraculous" recovery. Because of this rapid initial progress, families often bring their child home with the expectation that progress will continue until the child reaches a full or almost complete recovery.

The cognitive recovery process for children continues over many years as the child's brain develops and matures. The effects of an earlier injury to any part of the brain may not become fully evident until that area develops and is challenged in the classroom. Changes in learning, executive skills and behavior are among the most common long-term effects of brain injuries among children. For the children with a brain injury, time "reveals" rather than "heals" all wounds.

Neurocognitive Stall

Recent research in the neuroscience and neurorecovery of children with traumatic brain injuries identifies two phases of immediate and latent recovery. The immediate phase is the period from the time of injury up to approximately one year. This is the period where the child

A young boy has a postoperative checkup after successful brain surgery. Rehabilitation services are less available to children than to adults.
(© Michelle Del Guercio/ Photo Researchers, Inc.)

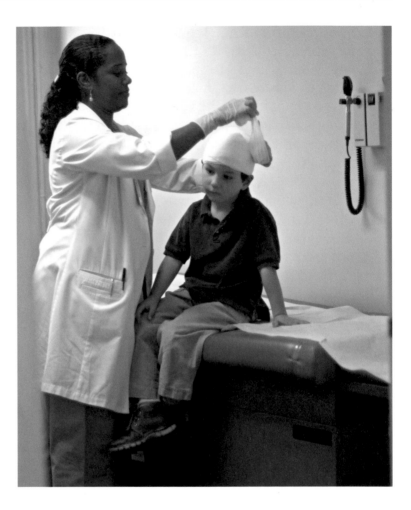

may receive emergency medical treatment followed by intensive hospital care and/or rehabilitation services. The latent recovery phase is the period from one year after the injury to years later, even up to young adulthood. It is during this later phase that the full impact of an injury to a child's developing brain becomes apparent.

Dr. Sandra Chapman [in a 2006 article] uses the term *neurocognitive stall* to describe ". . . a halting or slowing in later stages of cognitive, social and motor development beyond a year after brain injury. Despite a remarkable recovery during the first year after a severe brain injury, the child may appear to 'hit a wall' or 'fail to thrive' in terms of continued cognitive growth. It is not so much that the child loses already acquired skills as it is a failure or lag in development of later emerging cognitive milestones."

Children with severe brain injury are at greatest risk for a neurocognitive stall. With the lapse of time, they appear to grow *into* rather than out of their deficits. This often becomes evident during adolescence when the frontal lobes have rapid rates of growth and development from age 13 up to age 25. School work becomes more complex and so do social pressures with adolescence. These youth may have new difficulties keeping up with classmates and peers as they struggle to reach more complex cognitive levels in the classroom and with homework.

A Lack of Access

Access to inpatient pediatric rehabilitation care is far more limited for children than for adults. The number of accredited pediatric brain injury rehabilitation programs available is simply far less than for adults. The more rapid physical recovery often seen in children during the initial stages of hospital care also makes it more difficult to obtain insurance approval for transfer to inpatient rehabilitation. The lighter size and weight of children also makes it possible for parents to care for children at home even when there are significant physical demands for caregiving.

Data from the National Pediatric Trauma Registry found that for those children discharged home from a trauma center, referrals for physical therapy, occupational therapy and speech/language therapy were common. However, less than 2% of children and adolescents diagnosed with head trauma were referred to special education services. Despite the fact that traumatic brain injury was added as a specific category to the Individuals with Disabilities Education Act in 1990, trauma discharge teams are underutilizing the education referral process.

> # FAST FACT
>
> A 2008 survey found that only 21 percent of fifty-six youths with traumatic brain injury were given formal hospital-to-school transition services.

When you combine the limited transition planning and referral patterns between medical and educational systems with the emergence of latent cognitive challenges, it creates a tremendous challenge for school systems as they become the critical arena for learning and cognitive rehabilitation for these children.

It has been a frustrating contradiction for many clinicians, families and advocates that despite the fact that traumatic brain injury is the leading cause of disability among children, they are considered a low incidence population by the US Department of Education. This is reflected in low number of students receiving special education services under the classification of traumatic brain injury in every state.

Unfortunately, the link between an earlier injury to the child's brain and emerging cognitive problems in school is often missed. Many factors contribute to this including . . .

- Poor transition planning between medical and educational systems
- Limited training and experience of educators with this population
- Inadequate screening and history taking to identify previous TBI
- Latent effects of brain trauma mistakenly attributed to emotional or behavioral disorders
- Misidentification of cognitive changes as attention disorders or learning disabilities

The Role of Therapists

"The challenge of addressing the latent developmental effects of childhood brain injuries is compounded by the fact that families often must assume the primary caregiving role and schools often become the sole providers of rehabilitation services. Neither families nor educators have been systematically prepared or trained for this role," [states A. Glang and M. Lash in a 2006 article in

Areas Commonly Affected by Traumatic Brain Injury in Children

• New Learning	• Motor—Gross
• Language—Receptive	• Social/Emotional/Behavioral
• Language—Expressive	• Motor—Fine
• Memory	• Processing Speed
• Attention	• Initiation
• Visual/Spatial	• Organization
• Reasoning	• Planning
• Sensory Processing	• Mental Flexibility

Taken from: "Sixteen Areas Commonly Affected," Traumatic Brain Injury Networking Team Resource Network. http://cokidswithbraininjury.com.

Brain Injury/Professional]. Therapists can have a pivotal role in helping educators and school staff recognize this neurocognitive stall after a brain injury. Therapists are more than clinical resources for the child. They can also serve as effective advocates and educators for families and school staff about the neurorecovery process.

There is no one TBI curriculum or set of strategies for students with brain injuries. Unlike the educational field where best practices have been developed based on extensive research on students with autism and learning disabilities, research on effective methods for educating and supporting students with brain injuries is still in the infant stages of development.

What is known, however, is that each brain injury is unique and so each educational program must be individualized to address the learning and social challenges presented after the TBI. Students can have difficulty with processes of attention, memory, planning, organization, pragmatic language and social interactions. Many of these skills are interdependent. Therapists and teachers must work as a team to address these issues in the functional daily activities of the classroom. Some ideas for support in the classroom include:

Strategies for helping attention and concentration:

- Reduce distractions in student's work area
- Divide work into smaller sections
- Ask student to orally summarize information just presented
- Use cue words to alert student to pay attention
- Establish nonverbal cueing system to remind student to pay attention

Strategies to help with organization:

- Provide additional time for review
- Give written checklist of steps for each task
- Assign person to review schedule at start of school day
- Practice sequencing material

Many therapists and teachers will recognize these strategies as techniques they already use with other students. They are not unique to students with brain injury. No one teaching program will apply to all students with brain injuries. By remediation, adapting instruction or modifying the environment, therapists and educators can help the student be more successful in the classroom.

Brain Injury Is a Factor in Social Ills Such as Chronic Homelessness, Alcoholism, and Learning Disabilities

Thomas M. Burton

Thomas M. Burton is a Pulitzer Prize–winning reporter in the *Wall Street Journal*'s Chicago bureau, covering the medical care, pharmaceutical, and medical device industries. In the following viewpoint, Burton discusses research strongly suggesting that traumatic brain injury is at the root of many social problems. He cites research done by the Mount Sinai School of Medicine, which found high rates of "hidden" head trauma when screening various populations in New York. In one study 82 percent of homeless men in New York had a childhood brain injury; another study found about half of students in learning disabilities programs had suffered a blow to the head. According to Burton, the accident is often forgotten by the time symptoms such as poor organization or difficulty performing routine tasks are noticed so that people often do not link the symptoms to the preceding head injury.

SOURCE: Thomas M. Burton, "Studies Cite Head Injuries as Factor in Some Social Ills," *Wall Street Journal*, January 29, 2008. Copyright © 2009 by Dow Jones, Inc. All rights reserved. Reproduced by permisison.

Researchers studying brain injury believe they've found a common thread running through many cases of seemingly unrelated social problems: a long-forgotten blow to the head.

They've found that providing therapy for an underlying brain injury often helps people with a variety of ills ranging from learning disabilities to chronic homelessness and alcoholism. If broadly verified, the findings could have a significant impact in dealing with such intractable difficulties.

That severe head injuries can lead to cognitive and behavioral problems is widely accepted. The U.S. Centers for Disease Control and Prevention [CDC] estimates 5.3 million Americans suffer from mental or physical disability that is due to brain injury.

What's new is the contention of some researchers that there are many other cases where a severe past blow to the head, resulting in unconsciousness or confusion, is the unrecognized source of such problems. "Unidentified traumatic brain injury is an unrecognized major source of social and vocational failure," says Wayne A. Gordon, director of the Brain Injury Research Center at Mount Sinai School of Medicine in New York, where much of the research is being done.

Hidden Head Trauma

Research by his team has consistently found high rates of "hidden" head trauma when screening various populations in New York schools, addiction programs and the general population. The CDC acknowledges its 5.3 million estimate is an undercount based on hospital admissions; it doesn't include people who sought no treatment for a severe blow to the head or who were sent home from a doctor's office or emergency room with little treatment.

Causes of brain injury can include bike and car accidents, sports concussions such as those suffered by professional football players, and abuse and falls that can date back to childhood. Doctors say about 85% of common falls in infancy don't produce long-term deficits, but that some do.

To be sure, it's difficult to connect with any certainty a long-ago blow to the head to memory and cognition problems years later. Other researchers point out that many people do recover completely from severe head injury, and mental problems arise from other causes. Moreover, Mount Sinai's findings haven't all been published, nor have they been widely evaluated at other institutions.

A Case of Undiagnosed Brain Injury

Mount Sinai's research involves people like Kate Gleason, a business-college instructor who over the course of a year lost her ability to read, keep her home orderly and even maintain friendships.

In 1998, Ms. Gleason tried to open a window in her New York apartment building's hallway, but the heavy top window fell and bashed her on the head. She was treated by doctors at a local hospital, who she says let her walk home and told her she'd be fine. But on the way back, she was still so confused she had to hang onto lampposts and buildings to keep from losing her way.

A slim, auburn-haired woman then in her mid-40s, Ms. Gleason kept teaching, but found that the bright lights and hectic office were overwhelming. She says she confided in a boss about her troubles and soon lost her job. After that, she made ends meet by returning to proofreading work, but she slowly withdrew socially.

She didn't pay bills on time. Her house was a mess. "Years and years went by, and I had lots of problems," she says. "I didn't know it was from the head injury. I just thought I had a clutter problem." By 1999, Ms. Gleason, who has a master's from Columbia University, was "so bad on the level of functioning as a college grad that I wanted to die." She had no idea why.

Diagnosis and Treatment

Then about two years ago, she got a strange letter from Mount Sinai: It asked if she was having trouble thinking or solving problems or if she became easily overwhelmed. It turned out Mount Sinai doctors were reaching out to people whose medical records showed a blow to the head. Ms. Gleason responded, and when researchers interviewed her, she began to sob, saying, "Life is just so hard."

On what was to be the first day of an attention and memory program, Ms. Gleason got lost in the maze of hospital hallways and began crying again. Once she found the site, she discovered she wasn't the only patient who got lost a lot, or who cried.

For five days a week for six months, she worked through five hours of attention exercises, reading articles to explain the main idea, interpreting charts and graphs, taking classes on how to take apart a problem and reduce it to smaller steps, writing mock "advice columns" on how to handle life issues.

At first, she found the work so intense she needed a break every 15 minutes. By a week later, she could concentrate a little longer. She completed the program in August 2006, eight years after the window struck her. Now she's studying to be a church-based counselor. "That program gave me my life back," she says.

The Homeless Have High Rates of Head Injury

A group for whom the research on undiagnosed head injuries could be especially relevant is the homeless. Assessments by Mount Sinai researchers of about 100 homeless men in New York found that 82% had suffered brain injury in childhood, primarily as a result of parental abuse.

An epidemiological study in 2000 was larger. Researchers went door-to-door in New Haven, Conn., interviewing 5,000 people, 7.2% of whom recalled a past blow to the head that was followed by unconsciousness or a period of confusion. In follow-up testing, the re-

Incidence of Selected Health Problems in the United States

An estimated 1.5 million Americans sustain a TBI each year, which is eight times the number of people diagnosed with breast cancer and thirty-four times the number of new cases of HIV or AIDS, according to the Centers for Disease Control and Prevention.

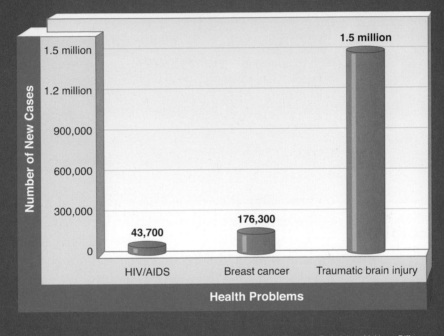

Taken from: "Incidence of Selected Health Problems in the United States." *Traumatic Brain Injury: Making a Difference Today*, Society for Neuroscience, 2005. www.sfn.org.

searchers found that those who reported such injuries had more than twice the rate of depression and of alcohol and drug abuse as others. They also had sharply elevated rates of panic disorder, obsessive-compulsive disorder and suicide attempts, say the researchers, led by Jonathan Silver of New York University.

Such research began in the late 1980s with Mount Sinai's Dr. Gordon and Mary Hibbard, both Ph.D. psychologists specializing in rehabilitation and neuropsychology. In questioning patients referred to them, they were struck

Recent studies indicate that approximately 80 percent of homeless men in New York City suffer from some kind of childhood brain injury. (© David Grossman/Alamy)

by how often they turned up a history of a brain injury that wasn't in the patients' medical records.

Using a questionnaire they devised, they tried to determine how many children in the city school system had head injuries that were followed by cognitive difficulties. At one school, 10% of students told of having once had a significant head injury. Later testing of these children frequently "was suggestive of impairments," Dr. Hibbard says.

Brain Trauma and Learning Disabilities

Next, with a grant from the U.S. Department of Education, they set out to determine how many pupils enrolled in programs for children with learning disabilities had ever suffered a hard blow to the head. The results were startling: About 50% had.

"The accident can be three months ago, but by the time the symptoms happen, the accident is forgotten. Nobody puts it together," says Tamar Martin, a psychologist in the program. The team worked with about 400 children, finding that many children who'd had brain injuries were lost in regular learning-disabilities classrooms.

They have trouble with their memory from day to day, and teachers can assume they're not trying hard, Dr. Martin says. They need more breaks between topics. But their performance varies greatly from day to day, and a teacher can also erroneously perceive this fluctuation as lack of initiative.

Just giving such children more time often helps, she says, as do special prompts from teachers. For instance, Dr. Martin says, a teacher may say, "In a couple of minutes, I am going to ask you about problem No. 10," and give the child time to prepare before officially asking.

One 14-year-old girl had a high intellect, but after she was hit by a car, she suddenly couldn't do outlines or organize her time, her mother says in an interview. "Her processing was slower," adds Michelle Kornbleuth, another psychologist in the Mount Sinai program. "She was frustrated, and her scores came out in the average range." With Dr. Kornbleuth's help, the girl was allowed to take exams privately in an office and could concentrate better. With such accommodations, she completed high school and went on to graduate from prestigious Smith College. . . .

> **FAST FACT**
>
> A 2010 study in Neuropsychological Rehabilitation noted that loss of consciousness from traumatic brain injury had occurred in 46 percent of young male criminal offenders.

The Mount Sinai team evaluates people via a battery of "neuropsych" tests lasting up to nine hours. They are shown pictures of objects, then asked minutes later what they saw. They see a complex geometric design with triangles, lines and circles and are asked to draw it from memory. They're shown a series of multiple random letters and asked to cross out, say, the "c" and "e" every time they see one. . . .

Many Addicts Have Suffered Head Injuries

About five years ago [in 2003] the Mount Sinai team began looking at residents of New York centers for alcoholism and drug abuse. They evaluated 845 patients and determined that 54% had once suffered a hard blow to the head. Of course, some had injuries after they began drinking, so there is a certain chicken-and-egg problem with that number.

Steven Kipnis, medical director of a New York state agency for alcoholism and addiction, says his work with counselors convinces him that many of the patients became alcoholic or addicted in part because of a head injury, and knowing about it helps in treatment.

"Someone can get hit in the head with a softball and still be working. They tend to be in denial. They get mood swings, they yell at a spouse. It's a slow downward spiral, and that's when alcohol and drugs" become an option, he says.

The agency has a program specifically for the brain-injured at the R.E. Blaisdell Addiction Treatment Center in Orangeburg, N.Y. A counselor there, Steve Oswald, tells of one patient who dropped out of a general alcoholism program three times before the program for the brain-injured began, and then successfully completed the program.

In 2006, Mount Sinai's Dr. Gordon began to work with Common Ground, a New York nonprofit that builds housing for the homeless. About 70% of 100 homeless people they tested came out in the 10th percentile or lower for memory, language or attention, says the group's director of psychiatric services, Jennifer Highley. Questioning uncovered that 82% had a significant blow to the head prior to becoming homeless, usually from severe parental abuse during childhood.

"People get abused as kids, making them inattentive in school and sometimes unable to learn," says Ms. Highley. She says head injury and the emotional fallout from abuse can lead to alcoholism and addiction, and "that combination creates the inability to function and often leads to homelessness."

Most Patients in Minimally Conscious or Persistent Vegetative States Should Have Life Support Discontinued

J. Andrew Billings, Larry R. Churchill, and Richard Payne

J. Andrew Billings is the founder and director of the Palliative Care Services at Massachusetts General Hospital and coauthor of *The Clinical Encounter*. Larry R. Churchill holds the Ann Geddes Stahlman Chair in Medical Ethics at Vanderbilt University and is the author *of Rationing Health Care in America: Perceptions and Principles of Justice*. Richard Payne is professor of medicine and divinity at Duke Divinity School, and the Esther Colliflower Director of the Duke Institute on Care at the End of Life. In the following viewpoint, the authors argue that reports claiming to find high degrees of consciousness in some stroke patients in minimally conscious states (MCS) or persistent vegetative states (PVS) are very misleading. According to the authors, scans of the brain may show activation of a particular brain region that is associated with a certain type of experience (e.g., imagining playing tennis), but that does not necessarily mean that the patient is consciously having that experience. However, they claim that there is a high likelihood that such patients, despite being in a deeply unconscious and impaired state, can continue to feel pain and discomfort.

SOURCE: J. Andrew Billings, Larry R. Churchill, and Richard Payne, "Severe Brain Injury and the Subjective Life," *The Hastings Center Report*, vol. 40, issue 30, May/June 2010, p. 17. Copyright © 2010 by The Hastings Center. All rights reserved. Reproduced by permission.

The experience of pain, they assert, is associated with more primitive brain structures that are likely to still be functional in a patient whose higher brain centers (and therefore ability to have a rich inner life) are severely damaged. They therefore advise that most PVS/MCS patients should have life support discontinued.

Recent neuroscientific developments challenge our familiar, intuitive understanding of basic mental phenomena such as consciousness, awareness, attention, reasoning, free will, and moral responsibility. The understanding of the brain now emerging is not easily grasped and may not even be explicable using familiar terms and concepts. Progress in the neurosciences potentially poses an even more dramatic transformation in how we think about ourselves than was precipitated by the Darwinian revolution. But we are only beginning to get a blurry appreciation of what the future holds.

One new method of studying the brain, functional magnetic resonance imaging (fMRI), has proved an extraordinary way to identify localized neural activity. Press reports often have a rather breathless quality. National Public Radio recently invoked mental telepathy with a story, "Computers One Step Closer to Reading Your Mind," in which we learn, "At the extreme, maybe we could decode somebody's dream while they are dreaming."

At least up until now, the neurological criterion for awareness has been observable responses to behavioral stimuli. New evidence suggests that a few patients diagnosed as being in a permanent vegetative state (PVS) or minimally conscious state (MCS)—conditions associated with severe brain injury and an absence of behavioral responses to external events—show signs on fMRI of reactivity to noxious stimuli and even to spoken words. This has led to the novel and radical idea that we might be able to communicate with patients who have suffered severe brain injury. A recent and much-discussed study by Martin M. Monti and colleagues, entitled "Willful Modulation of Brain Activity in Disorders of Consciousness" and published in the *New England Journal of Medicine* [NEJM], states that "in a minority of cases, patients who meet the behavioral criteria for a vegetative state have residual cognitive function and even conscious awareness . . . the functional MRI data provided clear evidence that the patient was aware and able to communicate." The paper concludes with the humane hope that we may eventually be able to establish reliable communications with patients with severe brain damage.

These studies are methodologically sophisticated, rest on a solid body of research, and have breathtaking implications. But they also beg for careful interpretation. . . . We will argue that premature, overreaching, and wildly reductionistic conclusions have been drawn, partly by ignoring major findings in contemporary brain research, and that highly important clinical implications have been overlooked. . . .

Consciousness and Neural Activity

Understanding the neurobiological basis of consciousness—the totality of the impressions, thoughts, and feelings that make up a person's awareness—is the holy grail of brain science. How can we understand our experience of perceiving and our sense of being central within this perceived world? As Antonio Damasio has put it, "With a few exceptions to the contrary, consciousness is presumed to be the most complex and impenetrable human property, from which follows that it is the most difficult to define and the most problematic to investigate."

Unfortunately, some interpretations of the fascinating new fMRI studies seem to conflate findings associated with willful consciousness with the actual occurrence of willful consciousness. Seams and ridges on a baseball are essential conditions for throwing a curveball, but confirming the presence of seams and ridges does not a curveball make. Likewise, showing that the impaired brains of some patients light up to the words, "imagine playing tennis," does not mean that the notion of tennis is part of their awareness or even that the patient made a conscious decision to follow the instructions. Willfulness is a manifestation of a person's mind, as are consciousness and awareness, while activation—the localized change in blood flow detectable by fMRI—is merely one function in the brain. . . .

Localization and the Unconscious

Modern neuroscience provides many findings about the complexity of brain function that should discourage us from jumping from evidence of local brain reactivity to conclusions about consciousness. Two major observations deserve mention.

Localization. The notion of localizing neurological functions in specific areas of the brain has a long and productive history in brain science and forms the basis for clinical diagnosis of many brain injuries. For instance, sensory changes in the left arm point to a lesion in a specific area of the brain. However, [according to Carl Zimmer in *The Soul Made Flesh:*]

> While the brain may be a collection of modules, none of them can work alone. During any mental task, information reverberates in a far-flung network of regions that light up like constellations on an fMRI scan. These networks are constantly changing over scales of seconds, minutes, and decades.

In the case of pain, multiple areas of the cerebral cortex and deeper brain structures, including emotional centers, are involved in a complex, interactive manner, working serially and in parallel along with both ascending and descending . . . messages transmitted along the spinal cord. Some sites in this brain matrix may be required for the perception of pain, while others may profoundly influence perception under particular cognitive, emotional, or physiological circumstances. As Irene Tracey and Emily Johns note, "when coordinated in activity the result is the multidimensional perception that is pain; a sensory, emotional, motivational and cognitive experience." Similarly, the visual system proves to be strikingly complex in its processing and interpretation of stimuli and in determining what information reaches consciousness. It also has the remarkable ability to "bind" or bring together a variety of data, transmitted along separate neurological tracts, into a single experience of seeing shape, color, texture, and movement. An fMRI study focused on a few areas of the brain cannot render the complexity of multiple areas of the brain communicating back and forth.

> FAST FACT
>
> According to the DANA foundation, there are as many as ten thousand children and twenty-five thousand adults in the United States in a persistent vegetative state.

The Unconscious. While we may perceive ourselves as willfully generating goal-directed actions, the vast majority of brain activity goes on without entering into our consciousness. The brain mostly "talks" to itself. This "talking" is essential neural activity but largely beyond our awareness. Consciousness and a sense of willfully carrying out an action or making a decision may even occur after the brain has initiated an action or decision. How will we distinguish conscious from unconscious neural activity on fMRI in these brain-damaged patients?

Consciousness and the Severely Damaged Brain

Consciousness, awareness, and will are challenging concepts in the realms of psychology, philosophy, theology, and law; equating experience with mere activation of brain sites is a fundamental mistake. Physiological processes in the brain are necessary for the emergence of consciousness, awareness, and will. Some commentators . . . doubt that consciousness can even be defined or that this utterly subjective "first-person" experience can ever be apprehended through the "third-person" methods of objective science. Consciousness is the medium through which human beings work and thereby systematically eludes precise definition or localization.

Making sense of the Monti study forces us to clarify and revise our fundamental notions of higher brain functions. Using terms like *awareness* or *consciousness* to describe brain functions in patients with severe brain injuries may be misleading. In commonsense terms, as well as in medical use, "awareness" suggests a quality of consciousness similar to normal but perhaps dampened, as in various levels of anesthesia or stages in the emergence from coma. But if even simple cognitive functions in normal subjects reflect highly complex interactions across a wide variety of brain sites, what kind of consciousness or awareness are we talking about when we consider patients with such extensive brain injuries? Relatively localized brain lesions can produce major neuropsychiatric dysfunction; we can only guess at the effect of widespread cerebral damage. Is there a continuum of awareness or are there different kinds of awareness, and when does consciousness become a meaningless term in such patients? Using a term like *awareness* to describe the cognitive experience of a patient with an extensive brain injury is like comparing the sensation of seeing a spot of white light to the experience of visiting the Louvre [Museum] with a loved companion and then enjoying a pleasant walk in the Tuileries [Gardens] on your way to a fine meal at a favorite restaurant. New language is needed to describe experiences when so much essential neurological function is destroyed. Our very notions of personhood are challenged.

Clinical Implications

One important but largely overlooked issue raised by these studies is the possibility that patients with severe brain injury—even those in PVS—have the capacity to suffer. Pain is a primitive phenomenon that is present in most, if not all, animal species. Jaak Panksepp and colleagues argue that the pain system is closely related to the affective system, which is encoded by phylogenetically [pertaining to evolutionary development] older brain structures, in contrast to neurological processes dependent on neocortical [more recently evolved part of the brain] activation. In PVS or MCS, after extensive neocortical damage but preservation of brainstem structures, pain is more likely to persist than consciousness. The notion that patients in PVS and MCS will communicate their wishes seems considerably less plausible than that they retain an ability to suffer.

Medicine has a venerable history of failing to address suffering. Pain is often minimized or ignored in clinical practice and remains under-recognized and undertreated. Only recently, for instance, has pain been properly recognized and addressed for such nonverbal persons as infants and patients undergoing neuromuscular blockade.

By definition, patients in PVS and MCS cannot communicate their feelings or indicate behaviorally that they are experiencing pain. By professional fiat and common clinical practice, they are viewed as not perceiving pain, or at least as having altered pain perception. Grimacing, moaning, and other behaviors suggesting distress are common in MCS and PVS, but neurologists do not count them as evidence of awareness because they are not localized. These patients may regularly undergo painful procedures and experience other discomforts (including those related to the initial injury), but they are totally helpless and probably receive very distorted input, if any, from the surrounding world. Routine neurological testing may also include use of very painful stimuli.

Impaired Patients May Experience Pain

A variety of studies now suggest that conditions of greatly impaired consciousness may be associated with pain. fMRI studies demonstrate patterns of response consistent with pain in PVS and especially MCS. Consider also that despite the massive, albeit temporary, disruption of cerebral processing that occurs in general anesthesia, as many as 0.7 percent of patients undergoing major surgery experience awareness, including pain, helplessness, fear, and panic.

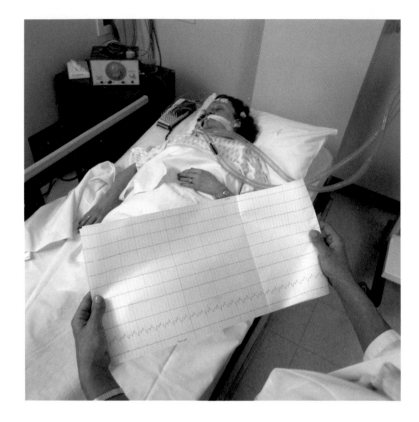

A nurse reviews the electroencephalogram of a "brain dead" patient. Many people believe that a person in a persistent vegetative state should have life support discontinued. (© Southern Illinois University/Photo Researchers, Inc.)

Published reports have not adequately addressed the possibility of suffering in these patients. Indeed, findings of neural activity in PVS patients in response to noxious stimuli directly contradict the American Academy of Neurology's opinion, dating from 1989 and renewed in 1994, that these patients do not experience pain. The International Association for the Study of Pain also fails to address concerns about suffering in PVS in its research guidelines. (In contrast, the 2002 definition of MCS describes "partial consciousness," and clinicians are advised that "the patient should be treated with dignity, and caregivers should be cognizant of the patient's potential for understanding and perception of pain."

For most of us, an immobile, bedbound, and possibly painful existence in which we are unable to communicate with others in the outside world or make sense of ourselves is material for a horror story, nothing like the rich, private world of Jean-Dominique Bauby's *The Diving Bell and the Butterfly*. How are we to be sure that such patients are not suffering? The daily clinical lesson seems to be that patients with severe brain injury should be carefully medicated, at least for physical suffering.

Of course, the question we would like to ask these patients, in addition to evaluating their discomfort, is whether they wish to remain alive and to be cared for in their present state. This is a question requiring not just consciousness but reflection, deliberation, and some knowledge of the context of one's condition. Someday, we may understand more about people with such damaged brains and may acquire some insight into what cognition is like for them and whether they are in distress. For now, when family members wonder about a patient's awareness, we can only express uncertainty and provide assurance that discomfort will be prevented or treated. For the foreseeable future, advance care directives and the substituted judgment of the family will be the guide for medical decision-making for the severely brain damaged, not an "objective" imaging procedure.

What fMRI May Really Say

Given the complexity of the system it attempts to understand, brain science is necessarily reductionistic. Simplified hypotheses (for example, that a particular fMRI pattern indicates awareness or that the failure of a pain signal to reach the cortex demonstrates that the patient did not experience the stimulus) are inevitable and necessary. But perceiving the inadequacy of these conclusions stretches us to devise better concepts and experiments. For fMRI studies, we should not mistakenly equate the "signal" for the "experience." . . .

There are important clinical lessons to be drawn from these fMRI studies. One is that our current way of classifying brain injuries is inadequate. Neither persistent or

Brain Regions Associated with Internal and External Awareness

Imaging studies have shown that particular areas of the brain are affected in unresponsive wakefulness syndrome/vegetative state patients. Some of these areas (shown in blue) are critical for internal awareness and others (red) are important for external, or sensory, awareness.

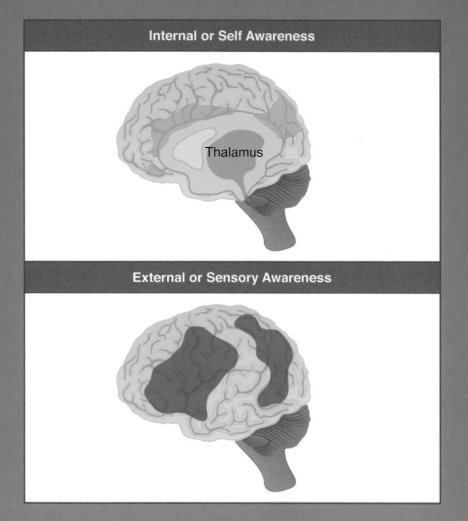

Internal or Self Awareness

Thalamus

External or Sensory Awareness

Taken from: V. Charland & S. Laureys. "Unresponsive Wakefulness Syndrome and Minimally Conscious State: Towards a Better Understanding of Disorders of Consciousness." International Brain Injury Association, 2011. www.internationalbrain.org.

permanent vegetative states nor MCS are . . . homogenous conditions, and while such terms may make sense now as clinical designations, further investigation with newer technologies will surely lead to finer distinctions and improved prognostication. We can anticipate many different patterns of impairment reflecting various combinations of localized injury.

We should also be cautious about overly pessimistic views of the future for severely brain-damaged patients. Significant errors in diagnosis of PVS from bedside test condition is supported by demonstrations of the plasticity of the nervous system and by technologies for stimulating the brain. At the same time, enthusiasm can be misleading, as in this description [from L. Naccache in a 2006 *Science* article] of a young woman who had spent five months in a vegetative state (not yet "permanent"): "Despite the patient's very poor behavioral status, the fMRI findings indicate the existence of a rich mental life, including auditory language processing and the ability to perform mental imagery tasks."

The potential for what most would call a meaningful or even marginal recovery for patients with PVS remains incredibly slim. Stories about a few remarkable cases of impressive recovery should not lead to an obligation to provide life-sustaining treatments. Given the extreme likelihood of unacceptably poor outcomes, most of these patients—as judged by their advanced directives or through substituted judgment—should have life support discontinued.

Life Support Should Not Be Discontinued for Most Patients in Minimally Conscious or Persistent Vegetative States

Dominic Lawson

Dominic Lawson is a British journalist. He is the former editor of the *Spectator* magazine and the *Sunday Telegraph* newspaper and writes a column for the *Independent*. In the following viewpoint, Lawson argues against the withdrawal of life support for patients who are diagnosed as being in a persistent vegetative state (PVS). According to Lawson, in many cases the patients have been misdiagnosed and are actually suffering from locked-in syndrome; that is, they are conscious but completely paralyzed. He details two cases in which such a misdiagnosis was made; in both cases doctors originally suggested discontinuing treatment but family members refused. Lawson also quotes the head occupational therapist of a hospital in London that specializes in neurodisability who states that 43 percent of their patients assessed as being in a PVS were later found to have been misdiagnosed. The author suggests that many patients who have been starved to death by court order must have been conscious.

It is remarkable how frequently we underestimate the most powerful force in the known universe: a mother's love. The story of Rom Houben is further proof, if proof were needed. Houben spent 23 years in what doctors regarded as an irreversibly vegetative state after a car crash at the age of 20. His mother, Fina Nicolaes, a nurse, was at all times convinced that her only son was sentient—alive, in the fullest sense of the word. Yet all the experts involved in Houben's care declared her son was simply a breathing cadaver. Nicolaes even took Houben to the United States, but there, too, she was told he was completely unresponsive.

In the end it was a specialist in their native Belgium, Steven Laureys of the coma science group at Liege University, who through a technique known as a tomography brain scan determined that Houben's cerebrum was functioning normally.

Thus encouraged, Laureys found Houben had some marginal movement in his right leg and by training that to push a button for "yes" and "no" re-established his patient's communication with the rest of the world. That was three years ago [in 2006]: now, after extraordinary efforts, Houben is able to use his right index finger to communicate via an electronic keyboard.

When he was visited by [the German periodical] *Der Spiegel*, which broke the story last week [in November 2009], the first journalist to see him asked the obvious question: "How did you survive for those 23 years, Mr Houben?" On the monitor the reply flashed up: "I meditated. I dreamt that I was somewhere else. And please call me Rom."

Locked-in Syndrome

It turns out that Houben was not in what doctors term a persistent vegetative state (PVS), but locked-in syndrome, the condition brought to global attention by Jean-Dominique Bauby's [1997 book] *The Diving Bell and the*

Butterfly. Houben, like Bauby, had kept his sanity—and even his enjoyment of life—by the power of imagination. Bauby wrote: "There is so much to do. You can wander off in space and time, set out for Tierra del Fuego or for King Midas's court." Condemned to nutrition via a nasogastric tube, the archetypal Frenchman Bauby recreated in his mind the wonderful flavours he had enjoyed in the past and everything associated with them. As one reviewer observed: "He reversed the most famous moment in [a work by Marcel] Proust and used the memory to bring back the madeleine."

For many, as they contemplate being in Houben's or Bauby's shoes, the idea of being locked in seems an unimaginable torment. It might as well be the 21st-century equivalent of the widespread terror of our ancestors—being buried alive, when catalepsy is misdiagnosed as death. [Nineteenth-century American author] Edgar Allan Poe's obsession with this gruesome idea created masterpieces of fictional horror which encouraged some of his contemporaries to install contraptions such as complicated alarm systems in their sarcophagi. This form of terror persisted long after the Victorian era: the novelist William Gerhardie, who died in 1977, requested his executors plunge a stake into his heart before he was interred—just in case.

Yet it is not the undiagnosed locked-in syndrome that Houben experienced which fills me with empathetic horror: it is the thought that if his mother had been less fiercely protective, she might have agreed to suggestions that the feeding tube be withdrawn "for his own sake." Then he truly would have been like a character out of Poe—starved to death, with the outside world oblivious to his inaudible screams.

This, after all, has been legal in the [United Kingdom] since Tony Bland, who suffered severe brain damage in the Hillsborough football stadium disaster, had his feeding tube withdrawn on February 22, 1993, after a decision by the law lords. Bland, who was not on a ventila-

Arousal and Awareness in Brain Death, Vegetative State, Minimally Conscious State, and Locked-In Syndrome

Two aspects of consciousness that can be observed in brain damaged patients are awareness and arousal. Both aspects are absent in coma and brain death. Patients in a vegetative state show arousal but no signs of awareness. The minimally conscious state involves fluctuations in both awareness and arousal. In locked-in syndrome, both aspects are present, but the patient experiences complete paralysis and inability to speak.

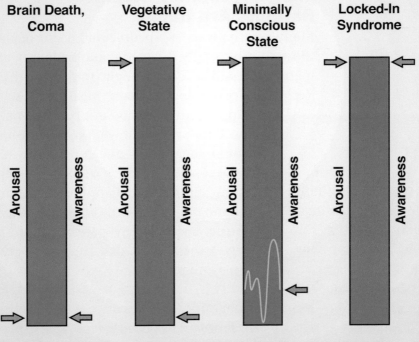

Taken from: C. Schnakers, J Giacino, and S. Laureys. "Coma: Detecting Signs of Consciousness in Severly Brain Injured Patients Recovering from Coma" [Figure 1]. In: J.H. Stone, M. Blouin, editors. *International Encyclopedia of Rehabilitation*, 2012.

tor and could breathe normally, took 10 days to die. It's interesting to contrast this case with the much less well known one of Andrew Devine, who suffered identical "crush" injuries to Bland in the same disaster, but whose parents refused to listen to the doctors' suggestions that his life was "over." He is back at home in Liverpool with his parents; his mother, Hilary, told a newspaper earlier this year [2009] that he can now be spoon-fed: "The medics were horrified that we fed him orally. . . . He can eat anything. He eats his breakfast, his dinner, his tea . . . he can understand what's going on—we know he can understand. He can make the people who know him best understand that he's uncomfortable or he's happy or he's unhappy."

Many Profoundly Disabled Patients Are Happy

Many—perhaps most—people find it unimaginable that those so profoundly disabled could be happy at all; even many professional carers might find it hard to believe. Yet when psychological tests measuring self-assessed happiness are carried out on such patients, the results are not at all what conventional wisdom would suggest. As one consultant in this specialised field told me: "Where zero is the middle of the happiness/unhappiness scale, minus five the most depressed and plus five the most euphoric, most of my patients indicate—when they are able to—that they are between plus three and plus four."

This, in America at least, should be of genuine political significance. Over there the story of Houben has been seized on by pro-life campaigners to reopen the case of Terri Schiavo, a comatose woman whose husband wanted her feeding tube withdrawn against the wishes of her parents: after seven years of legal battles, his will prevailed in the courts; 13 days after her feeding [tube] was withdrawn, Schiavo, 41, finally expired on March 31, 2005.

While those who fought to keep Schiavo alive now say the Houben case raises the awful prospect that she

> **FAST FACT**
>
> The sedative zolpidem partially restored brain function to several patients who had been in persistent vegetative states for several years, according to a study published in the journal *Neurorehabilitaiton* in 2006.

was fully aware of her fate, those on the other side of the argument say it proves the case for what they term "active euthanasia"—and what some of us would call murder. Jacob Appel, the bioethicist, wrote that "such calamities offer a compelling argument for withdrawing care. . . . [I would] regard Houben's fate as medically induced torture—I'd hope that my family would press a pillow over my face until my breathing stopped." Oddly enough, Houben does not share Appel's view that his mother should have stuffed a pillow over his face.

The case against turning off life support is exemplified by Rom Houben (pictured), who spent twenty-three years in a diagnosed vegetative state that was really caused by locked-in syndrome. (© AP Images/Yves Logghe)

Sentient Patients Starved to Death

It may well be that only those with a strong will to live survive a locked-in condition for any length of time. In 2005 the *British Medical Journal* (BMJ) published the account of a New Zealander called Nick Chisholm, who suffered similar trauma to Houben in a rugby accident. Chisholm recalled: "Without them knowing that I could still hear, the doctors and specialists in front of me said to my mum that I would die. They even asked my mum if she wanted them to turn the lifesupport system off after a few days. . . . I've always thought, f*** what they think and say—or I would have been dead at the start . . . don't will for death: it will come to you."

I am chilled by the thought that for every Houben or Chisholm or Devine with mothers able to fight their corner, there are many more whose parents are less doughty when faced by men in white coats telling them their children's bodies are devoid of function—except as organ donors.

Fortunately there are specialists who take a different approach, notably those at the Royal hospital for neuro-disability in Putney, southwest London. Last week [mid-November 2009] Helen Gill-Thwaites, its head occupational therapist, commented on the Houben case: "Astonishingly, we discovered that 43% of patients assessed [by us] had [also] been wrongly diagnosed as being in a PVS, with serious implications for their care, including the removal of life support."

Let's be clear: Gill-Thwaites is saying that sentient humans are being deliberately starved to death by court order because of persistent misdiagnosis and a crudely utilitarian approach. That's the real horror story.

Sexual Relationships with Brain-Injured Patients Present Ethical Dilemmas

The Hastings Center Report, Kristi L. Kirschner, Rebecca Brashler, Rebecca Dresser, and Carol Levine

The *Hastings Center Report* is a publication of the Hastings Center, a nonpartisan research institution dedicated to bioethics and the public interest. Kristi L. Kirschner is a professor of clinical medical humanities and bioethics at Northwestern University. Rebecca Brashler is an assistant professor of physical medicine and rehabilitation at Northwestern's Feinberg School of Medicine. Rebecca Dresser is professor of ethics in medicine at Washington University School of Law and the author of *When Science Offers Salvation: Patient Advocacy and Research Ethics.* Carol Levine is the director of the United Hospital Fund's Families and Health Care Project. In the following viewpoint, the *Hastings Center Report* describes a controversial case in which a husband (referred to as "Mr. Z") had intercourse with his severely brain-damaged spouse ("Mrs. Z"), resulting in a pregnancy that could endanger her health and leading to charges of rape by the woman's brothers. Various ethical considerations arising from the case are examined by the different authors. For example, Kirschner and Brashler suggest that if adults with a severe disability do not lose the right to accept or refuse medical treatment,

SOURCE: Kristi L. Kirschner, Rebecca Brashler, Rebecca Dresser, and Carol Levine, "Sexuality and a Severely Brain-Injured Spouse," *The Hastings Center Report,* vol. 40, issue 3, May/June 2010, pp. 14–16. Copyright © 2010 by the Hastings Center. All rights reserved. Reproduced by permission.

then they should be considered to retain the right to consent or reject the opportunity to enjoy intimate contact with their spouse. On the other hand, Dresser argues that Mrs. Z, in her minimally conscious state, is not capable of giving legally valid consent to intercourse. According to Levine, a primary consideration is Mr. Z's need to accept that his relationship with his wife has changed; he now needs to consider his primary role as one of caretaker, with a need to protect her from harm.

Mrs. Z is a twenty-nine-year-old woman who sustained a severe traumatic brain injury five years ago [in 2005] when she was hit by a car whose driver was drunk. She spent six months recovering, first in the hospital and then in a rehabilitation facility. Since her discharge from the rehabilitation facility, she has been living at home with her husband and her four-year-old twin sons. Mrs. Z is unable to speak, dependent in all mobility and personal care, incontinent, and has a feeding tube. Although alert and able to respond to visual, auditory, and tactile stimuli, Mrs. Z is clearly unable to participate in even basic decisions. She requires twenty-four-hour care.

A few months ago, Mrs. Z suffered abdominal discomfort, and her doctor discovered that she was pregnant. The pregnancy was terminated after physicians consulted on her case and determined that continuing it would compromise her health. Mrs. Z's parents are deceased, but her two older brothers have accused Mr. Z of rape. They contacted the local police asking that criminal charges be filed and have retained a lawyer to begin guardianship proceedings. Based on their sister's severe cognitive impairments, they do not believe that Mrs. Z can make any reasonable sense of what is happening to her and think that any sexual contact with a minimally conscious woman is inappropriate. They believe Mr. Z is abusive and his views self-serving.

Mr. Z is adamant that his wife would have wanted to maintain a physical relationship with him and that what takes place in the privacy of their bedroom is not something that should interest the probate courts or the police.

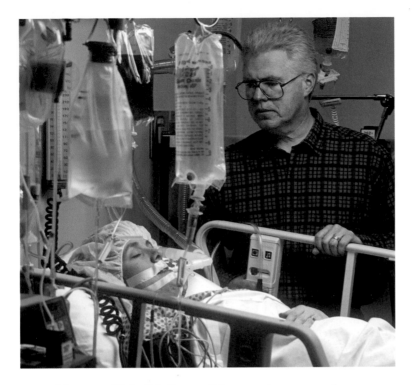

Sexual relations between partners when one is brain damaged has created ethical dilemmas.
(© Mira/Alamy)

As evidence of his fidelity to his marriage vows he argues that he did not divorce his wife when she became disabled and that he still loves her and finds her attractive.

A guardianship agency is reviewing the case for the judge and asks consultants to give their opinions on these questions: Does Mrs. Z's inability to provide consent to sexual intercourse override Mr. Z's claims of marital privacy? Does Mrs. Z's prior sexual relationship with her spouse constitute clear and convincing evidence that she would want her partner to continue this relationship, even if she is only a passive participant? Should Mrs. Z remain with her husband, or should her brothers be given the authority to remove her from her home?

First Commentary

Kristi L. Kirschner and Rebecca Brashler: While conversations about sexuality after disability are commonplace in rehabilitation, this particular case is unlike any we can recall. It is not like those of patients after spinal cord injuries, where the focus is on changed physiology, fertility, and ways to rediscover intimacy. It is unlike cases involving patients with developmental disabilities that prompt us to assess their understanding of sexuality and the consequences of intercourse and their ability to protect themselves from unwanted sexual advances. It is also unlike cases involving patients with severe cognitive disabilities who live in institutions—such as the young girl in a vegetative state who was raped by a staff member—where we address protection. Discussions about sexuality with the spouse of a person who is unconscious, minimally conscious, or as severely brain injured as Mrs. Z rarely occur.

That doesn't mean, though, that we don't discuss physical touch. We encourage family members to help range and massage stiff limbs, for example, and to show their loved ones affection. We teach family caregivers to participate with catheterization and bowel programs. But initiating a frank discussion about sexuality has not felt appropriate with these couples. This case makes us question the wisdom of that practice because of the risks associated with pregnancy and the possibility of rape charges.

In reality, we don't know much about the normative sexual practices of couples when one member has a severe brain injury. How often does sexual contact occur? Do spouses hope, as popular literature might lead us to believe, that the power of their touch might "awaken" the injured brain? Current research may shed light on this.

Sexual Consent Is Ambiguous

The question of capacity to consent is enormously difficult in this kind of situation. Consent typically involves verbal communication, while intimacy often involves subtle nonverbal cues. The Alzheimer literature tells us that when couples have been together for years, the fa-

> **FAST FACT**
>
> Several studies have found that more than half of those with traumatic brain injury report disruption to their sexuality after the injury.

miliar patterns of physical intimacy may be a comfort—a source of support and reassurance amidst an otherwise frightening and disruptive disease.

In this case it seems critical to balance Mrs. Z's privacy, best interests, and need for protection. Does she recognize her husband and welcome his sexual advances? Short of videotaping them in the privacy of their bedroom, we cannot think of a way to discern whether intercourse is consensual, or at least not harmful. We know she cannot take steps to protect herself, and that by allowing her to become pregnant, her husband was at least negligent. But is his negligence criminal? Is it substantial and grievous enough to remove her from his care forever?

Putting aside concerns about pregnancy, if severely disabled adults do not lose the right to refuse or accept medical care due to cognitive impairment (via substituted judgment and best interest standards of proxy decision-making), it seems logical that they also do not lose the right to refuse or accept the opportunity to engage in intimate contact with a spouse. Premorbid wedding vows and a sexual history with a spouse may constitute clear and convincing evidence that the individual desired a physical relationship with their partner. Having a spouse who believes that he married for better or worse, and could seek divorce but does not, seems like a blessing—exactly what many of us would hope for if we sustained a severe brain injury. In the end, assuming that Mrs. Z does not show fear or evidence of negative behaviors in the presence of her husband, we favor giving them a second chance with some safeguards in place due to the patient's vulnerable status.

Second Commentary

Rebecca Dresser: This case presents two major legal questions. One is whether the law would classify Mr. Z's actions as sexual assault. Many U.S. jurisdictions have rejected the old rule that rape cannot occur in a marriage. One rationale for the old rule was that consent to marry signified consent to intercourse throughout the marriage. That reasoning is now questioned, with many arguing that married women should have the same right as single women to decide about each instance of sexual contact.

Nevertheless, her severe mental disability leaves Mrs. Z incapable of giving valid consent to intercourse The legal standard for consent varies among the states, but at minimum, a woman must be able to understand the physical nature of the sexual act and that she has a right to refuse to engage in it. Underlying the concern about capacity to consent is knowledge that people with mental disabilities can be exploited by individuals seeking sexual gratification.

On the face of it, Mr. Z's actions could constitute sexual assault under the law. Nevertheless, I believe that few prosecutors would pursue charges in this situation. There is no clear evidence of physical or psychological harm to Mrs. Z from the encounters. And although it could be self-serving, Mr. Z's explanation for his behavior provides a plausible alternative story to exploitation. If we take him at his word, he believed intercourse was part of their relationship and was consensual in some sense. Although one can argue that this belief was unreasonable, the story he tells makes it possible to distinguish this case from the conduct targeted by sexual assault laws.

Substituted Judgment and Best Interest

The remaining legal question is whether Mrs. Z should be cared for at home or somewhere else. Two standards are available to assist in resolving this question. The substituted judgment standard seeks to determine what the impaired individual would choose if she were capable of decision-making and aware of her current circumstances. To apply the standard, we must consider whether the evidence about Mrs. Z's beliefs and behavior before her injury points to a particular result.

The available evidence fails to tell us much about what Mrs. Z would choose, however. Her prior sexual behavior fails to indicate whether she would prefer to continue

Common Changes to Sexual Behavior Following Traumatic Brain Injury

Reduced libido	About half of people with traumatic head injury experience a drop in sex drive. The remainder experience increased libido or no change at all.
Erectile problems	Between 40 and 60 percent of men have either temporary or permanent impotence following their injury.
Inability to orgasm	Up to 40 percent of men and women report difficulties having an orgasm.
Reduced frequency of sex	Some of the possible reasons include disability, depression, relationship breakup, and sexual problems.

Taken from: "Traumatic Brain Injury and Sexual Issues," Better Health Channel. www.betterhealth.vic.gov.

a sexual relationship with her husband in this drastically different situation. And because of his personal interests in the matter, we cannot rely solely on Mr. Z's claim that she would want to continue having a sexual relationship with him.

When substituted judgment fails to supply clear answers, the best interest standard comes into play. Case law on sterilization for individuals with mental disabilities offers guidance on how to think about Mrs. Z's placement. In those cases, courts consider the potential benefits and harms of the procedure and compare them to the potential benefits and harms of available alternatives, such as long-term contraception. They choose the approach that would produce the greatest net benefit from the disabled woman's perspective.

In deciding where Mrs. Z should live, the judge should consider the potential benefits and harms of keeping her at home, as well as the potential benefits and harms of placing her in another setting. This will require an evaluation of how Mrs. Z responds to her husband and children and how she responds to other potential caregivers. If her behavior suggests that she is most content with Mr. Z and the children, the judge could reasonably allow her to remain at home on a trial basis. With close monitoring to protect Mrs. Z's welfare, keeping her at home could be the best alternative.

Third Commentary

Carol Levine: The language of ethics sits uneasily in the realm of intimate human relationships. Describing sex as a partner's duty, obligation, right, or any other normative word seems both to diminish its meaning and elevate it to an unchallengeable principle. Even the word consent seems misapplied in this context; it implies that one person asks and the other accedes to the request. Nor does the language of science work much better. Locating the pleasure centers in the brain stimulated by sexual activity (and chocolate?) may tell us something about cognition but not much about how to live one's life as a person with a brain injury, or as that person's partner. We lack the words—and, more important, we lack the wisdom—to know what enhances human dignity and respect in these situations.

The essence of the sexual relationship between loving partners is not a contract, a vow in perpetuity, or a mechanical physiological response but a complex expression of their mutual commitment, love, and passion for each other. Sex in a marriage changes over time and often deepens in meaning as it decreases in frequency. Certainly illness and disability create the need for sensitive accommodation to the new reality. Serious brain injury is particularly challenging because it involves not a different body, but a very different self. Mrs. Z will never be the person she used to be. Her body may appear the same, but her ability to understand her identity and the way in which others can relate to her has changed.

Brain Trauma Changes a Relationship

Mr. Z does not seem to have accepted his wife's altered state and what that means for their relationship. He continues to see himself as her lover, when his primary responsibility to her now is to protect her from harm, enhance the quality of her life as much as possible, and add her responsibilities as a parent to his own. He has clearly violated the first responsibility by failing to protect her from a pregnancy that could compromise her health. Was he perhaps hoping for a miracle? Does he really believe that "finding her attractive" makes his actions more acceptable? Divorce is not the only alternative. Some people in this situation are able to maintain their caregiving responsibilities only because they find companionship and intimacy outside the marriage. Mrs. Z's brothers, however, have compounded the problem by their actions. Are there other sources of their fury? Was this tension with Mr. Z part of the family dynamics throughout the marriage, or perhaps even earlier?

At its core this case is not about sex. It is about control. And it is a family tragedy, not just an individual or marital tragedy. Who is looking out for the interests of the couple's two children? They have lost the love and nurturing of their mother; their father is engaged in a bitter legal battle with their mother's family. How does this affect them emotionally?

Whatever legal decision is reached about Mrs. Z's custody and placement, there should be a plan in place to counsel the whole family, separately if need be and ultimately as a unit. Perhaps a mediator or other trained professional could assist them in putting aside their individual interests to provide a stable, loving environment for the children. If Mr. Z agrees that he is responsible for protecting the vulnerable people in his care, I would favor keeping Mrs. Z at home. Whether Mrs. Z as she is now would want to have sex with her husband or not, she would surely want her family to come together for the sake of her children.

CHAPTER 3

Personal Experiences with Traumatic Brain Injury

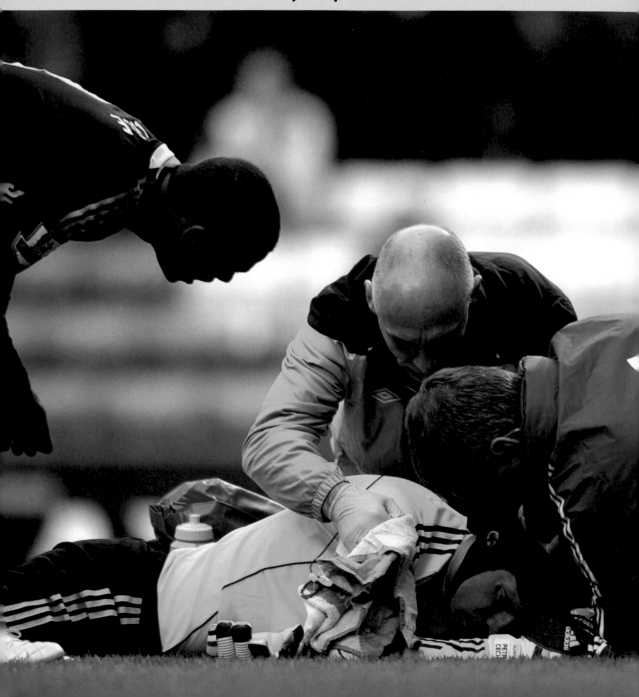

A Former High School Athlete Describes the Effect of Two Sports-Related Concussions

Caitlin Monaghan

Caitlin Monaghan is a former high school athlete. In the following viewpoint taken from her congressional testimony, Monaghan describes several concussions she experienced in high school. Her first concussion happened in grade seven and resulted in only mild symptoms; however, in her senior year two concussions within a short interval had a more serious impact on her life.

I had been a dedicated athlete all my life, playing both basketball and soccer from the time I was 6 years old. I loved being active and even more loved being part of a team. In many ways, being a serious athlete was expected in my town. Parents and children crowded the fields starting from Saturday mornings up until Sunday nights and as we got older our school weeks were filled with long practices and games.

SOURCE: Caitlin Monaghan, "Prepared Statement of Caitlin Monaghan, Former High School Athlete," *The Impact of Concussions on High School Athletes: The Local Perspective: Field Hearing Before the Subcommittee on Communities,* Committee on Education and Labor, US House of Representatives, 111th Congress, 2nd session, U.S. Government Printing Office, September 13, 2010, pp. 21–22.

Photo on facing page. A soccer player who has sustained a head injury is attended to during a match. The danger of even minor concussions is that they may cause problems that only arise later in life. (© Shaun Botterill/ Getty Images)

It was in 7th grade when I experienced my first concussion. I had been tripped in a soccer game and ended up on the ground only to have an opposing player kick me in the head. Though today I don't remember all the details of what my parents did or what my coaches did, I do remember suffering from headaches and experiencing sensitivity to light for a few weeks. I rested and was back on the field ignoring any laboring symptoms.

It was not until my senior year of high school when I realized the severity of the situation when it comes to concussions. It was the fall and our soccer team was playing our biggest rival. To say my teammates and I were pumped up would be an understatement. We knew that they would be aggressive and fight for every loose ball and commit to every ball tackle. We had to do the same to win.

In the second half, I ran to stop an oncoming shot on goal, which was kicked from no more than 7 feet away and received a blow to the side of the head. Within seconds I felt disoriented and hit the ground experiencing a black out. Play was not stopped right away because my team did not have possession of the ball. The coaches eventually came onto the field. They asked me a series of questions to see if I was alert. I was brought to the sideline, given an ice pack and checked on once or twice. Lying there I felt nauseous, disoriented and had a pounding headache. I was not in the condition to go back with the team on the bus, so a mother drove me directly home and told my parents about what happened. I missed the following day of school due to a severe headache and dizziness.

Second Shock Syndrome

The symptoms continued over days; simply put I just didn't feel like myself. My mother took me to my pediatrician to get an opinion. He was very concerned and thus recommended I see a neurologist.

The neurologist ran all the necessary tests and concluded that I had in fact suffered a mild to severe concussion. I was prohibited from playing sports until my symptoms subsided. I was to see him for further checkups as well as work with my high school's athletic trainer to track my symptoms. I was also alerted of the dangers of second shock syndrome and other consequences if I were to get hit again.

My world was playing sports and sitting on the sidelines was not enough. After two weeks, I started to try light running and though the headaches and dizziness continued, I ached to get back to playing. To be honest, the pressure to play again was increasing. It was hard to convince my coaches that I was still injured, because when they saw me in school I was laughing and talking with my friends, I seemed fine. My teammates also wanted me back and questioned when I would return. I was back to full play within 3 weeks of the first concussion even though I was not 100%. Headaches lasted through practice and often my sight was blurry. But it was my senior year and since I was not going to continue with soccer in college, I wanted to give everything I had left in me, my coaches and teammates deserved that.

> **FAST FACT**
>
> The Center for Injury Research and Policy estimates that 146,000 high school athletes suffered concussions during the 2008–2009 school year, increasing to 187,000 the following year.

It was during a scrimmage at one of my first practices back when I received another concussion. I went to block a shot on goal and once again got a blow to the side of the head. Feeling very dizzy, I managed to reach the side of the field where I laid down on a bench. My coaches told me to rest. My athletic trainer was notified and rushed to the field. She gave me ice, asked me questions and told me to remain lying down. My parents were contacted and I went home.

My trainer notified [me] that because of the time that had elapsed between both concussions I could no longer play. I was devastated. Though I attended every practice and cheered at every game till the end of the season, I no longer felt part of the team.

The Effects Become More Noticeable

We returned to the neurologist and he ran more tests and concluded that after two concussions continuing with any physical activity would be dangerous. I was to rest and focus on letting my brain heal. It was from the time of the second concussion through winter break that I really noticed the effects of my concussions on my schoolwork. The headaches and sensitivity to light along with a loss of concentration made it hard to pay attention. My mother remembers me being very tired and not myself. I had been a good student, but my grades started to slip a little. Though my teachers had known that I was injured, I don't think they realized how long the symptoms persisted. I participated less and found it hard to concentrate on my homework, especially after trying to force myself to concentrate through the entire school day.

Come January, I pushed to play basketball believing that I was well rested and healed. I was team captain, and though I was captain during my junior year as well, I felt that this was my year to lead my team. My trainer agreed to keep an eye on me. I could participate in warm-up drills and over time could play more and more as long as I was symptom free.

In truth, I was not symptom free. The fast running and jumping that comes along with basketball just brought on worse headaches. I would experience blurry vision and dizziness. I kept playing and if it got bad I would ask to sub out for a quick rest. I did however realize that aggressive play during games could lead to an elbow to the head or I could be tripped and hit my head on the floor and thus I started to become very apprehensive. I would not be as aggressive under the hoop and held back to taking a charge. I was not playing my best and therefore my coach did not play me.

Lingering Effects

It was difficult to tell my basketball coach that the two concussions I suffered during soccer were still bothering me and that that was the reason I was not playing my best. He had been told about the incidents, but did not pay too much attention to the ramifications. He had been a high school and college football player and thus concussions to him were a normal injury that required a little rest. I once again sat cheering from the sideline.

Though my senior year was wonderful and a time that I look back on with joy, I know that those two concussions made a huge impact on my life. On top of the symptoms that eventually eased, I had watched two sports seasons end from the bench, had a hard time concentrating in school, affecting my grades, and above all had felt that I had let many people down. I left for college knowing that I would not play sports at a collegiate level and was even wary to kick around a soccer ball or shoot hoops with my friends at school.

Today, I am fine. My world has expanded far beyond soccer and basketball, but when I hear the stories of people who have suffered from concussions I am reminded of my own story. I believe we need to do a better job advocating for the athlete and it starts with educating every party involved; parents, coaches, athletic trainers, teachers, school nurses and the athletes themselves.

A Mother Describes Caring for a Child with Traumatic Brain Injury

Dixie Coskie, posted by Tripp Underwood

Dixie Coskie is a fund-raiser, public speaker, advocate for the disabled, and a mother of a child who suffered a severe traumatic brain injury. She is the author of *Unthinkable: A Mother's Tragedy, Terror, and Triumph Through a Child's Traumatic Brain Injury*. In the following viewpoint, Coskie describes the impact her thirteen-year-old son's severe traumatic brain injury had on her and her husband as they took on the role of primary caregivers for him in addition to raising their other children. According to Coskie, she eventually developed health problems of her own as a result of caregiver burnout. She relates how she learned to balance taking better care of herself while continuing to give care to loved ones in need.

SOURCE: Dixie Coskie, "One Patient's Story: Caring for the Caregiver," *Thriving: Children's Hospital Boston's Pediatric Health Blog*, June 28, 2010. http://childrenshospitalblog.org. Copyright © 2010 by Dixie Coskie. All rights reserved. Reproduced by permission. Please visit www.dixiecoskie.com.

No one is immune to getting that phone call—the one that tells you something bad has happened to your family. Be it a diagnosis of a life-threatening disease or an involvement in a horrific accident, you never expect it to happen to someone you love. When it does, most of us are totally unprepared for the constant caregiving that follows and how it can impact your life emotionally, spiritually and physically.

I received such a call in 2001 when my 13-year-old son was involved in a bike accident without a helmet. Among many other severe injuries, he incurred traumatic brain injury. Not expected to live, Paul was given last rites. Doctors warned me that if he did survive, his quality of life would be questionable. Finally, Paul woke from a two-month coma. He couldn't walk, talk or perform the simplest of tasks.

Suddenly, in addition to taking care of the needs of my other seven children, with ages ranging from 6 to 16, I needed to learn medical techniques used in caring for a severely handicapped child. My husband and I worked as a nonstop team, one of us caring for the rest of the household while the other took care of Paul at a rehab hospital an hour from our home. In the shuffle, there was no time for us to take care of our own needs. The caregiving was isolating, demanding and never-ending.

Caregiver Burnout

A year after the crash, my son healed enough to be able to return to school in a wheelchair. These were my first moments of reprieve. My mind and body now had time to register what we'd been living through—all the fear, exhaustion and stress—and I collapsed under the strain. The pain shooting through my body was excruciating. My husband and children once again faced the dread of medical uncertainty. I saw a neurologist and endured numerous invasive tests to identify the mystery pain, but results were inconclusive. Possibly I had multiple sclerosis, or bone spurs in my neck or fibromyalgia. I saw a rheumatologist to check for Lyme disease, arthritis and lupus. I was put on a high dose of pain medications, which left me groggy and dizzy. I was desperate to get better and get back to caring for Paul and the rest of my family.

A specialist in Boston finally diagnosed my condition: post-traumatic stress syndrome and something called thoracic outlet syndrome. My doctor recommended counseling because she thought I may have been experiencing caregiver burnout. She also recommended physical therapy to help decompress the muscle tension around my shoulders and upper arms, which had become incredibly tight because of all the stress.

After four years of speech, occupational and physical therapy, Paul was walking, talking and taking steps once thought impossible. But then during his junior year of high school, a new and unrelated medical problem surfaced; Paul was diagnosed with leukemia. I knew another enormous fight was in front of us, with lots of procedures and hospital stays. Paul was scared but bravely prepared himself for another round of long hospital stays and doctor visits. . . .

> **FAST FACT**
>
> Each year in the United States about 180 children per 100,000 suffer a traumatic brain injury, according to a 2008 article in *Pediatrics for Parents*.

Taking Care of the Caregiver

Because of our first catastrophic medical experience I knew this time I needed to take care of myself in order to be able to take care of Paul and my family. I sought out positive people for support. I took breaks from the hospital to exercise, meditate or just have a moment to myself. I realized that asking for help was not a weakness, and when friends asked what they could do, I gave them a list of chores like shopping, carpooling and meal preparation. I rid myself of guilt and acknowledged my strengths. I educated myself on the diagnoses and worked to improve the line of communication with family and friends.

Those of us who have had a brush with death, catastrophic injury or illness realize more deeply how fleeting life is. Tell others how much you love them, and tell them often. Try to never take anyone for granted. Choose to react to your situation with a sense of faith, hope, patience, humor, passion and a lot of love. Be realistic about what you can and cannot do and take care of yourself along the way.

A Musician's Life Is Changed Forever After Being Shot in the Head

John W. Cassidy

John W. Cassidy is a neuropsychiatrist and former Harvard Medical School faculty member, who founded the traumatic brain injury program at Boston's McLean Hospital. In the following viewpoint, Cassidy tells the story of John Stambino, a musician who was shot in the head as a bystander in a convenience store robbery when he was thirty-one years old. Symptoms of Stambino's injury, which damaged much of the right hemisphere of his brain, included loss of memory, inability to perceive the left side of his body, obsessive-compulsive disorder, uncontrollable crying, and impulsive behavior. Cassidy describes how these deficits affected Stambino's life and how he was able to eventually get help for some of his symptoms through a residential brain-injury treatment program.

SOURCE: John W. Cassidy, *Mindstorms: The Complete Guide for Families Living with Traumatic Brain Injury.* New York: Da Capo Press. 2009, pp. 40–46. Copyright © 2009 by Da Capo Press. All rights reserved. Reproduced by permission.

A new self for John Stambino, a thirty-one-year-old musician, was born in an act of senseless violence in 2000, when he and his band buddies went to a convenience store to get some snacks before they went to play at a club. They were in the store when a gunman wearing a ski mask came in with a loaded .38 semiautomatic. When the clerk did not respond fast enough to demands for cash, the gunman started shooting; he killed five people and injured several more before killing himself. One of John's band members was killed and John was severely injured when he was shot in the head. He survived his injury and was taken to a nearby trauma center for treatment.

John lay in a coma for six days. His new life began with a series of operations that led to the loss of three-quarters of his right frontal lobe. Then came the residual symptoms of his gunshot wound: the inability to walk, the crying that wouldn't stop, the loss of memory. Widespread damage to the right side of his brain where the bullet exited his skull left him incapable of sensing the left side of his body. When he later learned how to shave again, he would shave only half his face; he didn't recognize the other half as being his face.

Impulse Control Problems

As his strength returned, John became obsessive-compulsive. He continually felt compelled to wash his hands, and he had to have everything ordered in a certain way. For example, he insisted on keeping nine of every item that he used in his daily activities, believing that if his world was held together by his lucky number his anxiety would decrease. When he could walk again, he had to go up and down the stairs literally nine times before he felt comfortable leaving the house; he had to count to nine before taking a bite of food, and he had to brush each region of his teeth nine times before going to bed. If he didn't, his anxiety escalated to the point where he couldn't contain it; the obsessive-compulsive disorder (OCD) led him to believe that something horrible would happen to his parents or to him if these rules were not followed.

"I know I'm different," he said. "But who cares? I can still get the job done." Unfortunately, he had many different jobs after leaving acute rehab: He could get jobs, but keeping them was an entirely different matter. John could follow workplace rules, but he could not always correctly understand them or manage to generalize a specific situation to more general patterns of behavior. And, of course, his stacked rows could only contain nine items in any one stack.

Besides the OCD, John had continual difficulties with impulse control. When his mother explained to him why he couldn't do or say certain things—why he couldn't scream at people, for example—John felt bad, often saying over and over again that he really didn't mean to do it. But he missed the connection between action and its regulation by thought, instead responding with his first impulses. He often had to be bluntly told that he was acting inappropriately, as he just couldn't objectively realize that his actions were disruptive to others. Of course, he was remorseful, but he truly did not realize the impact of his behavior on others. He never planned to be disruptive; it was just what happened when he felt an emotional impulse and expressed it without conscious thought as to its consequences.

Determined to Get Better

After coming to terms with his repeated failures, John was determined to get better and, for a brief, shining moment in time, it looked like he would. A year after leaving his first rehabilitation facility, John reunited with his uninjured band members and two new players to perform at a well-known rock club in New York City, where they put on a benefit concert to help raise money for John's rehabilitation. He played his guitar, a skill that he had retained despite his other deficits, as his prior motor memory in this area was unaffected. Once he got into the groove and no longer had to think about what he was doing, he really began to rock, and the crowd went wild. As the band concluded its performance by playing "We Are the Champions," people began dancing in the aisles, singing along, feeling the miracle of the John they used to know seemingly restored.

But the dream was shattered only two weeks later. During a band rehearsal, John had a severe seizure associated with flashing lights and fell from the stage, striking his head, and had to be rushed to the ER [emergency room]. His hopes of returning to his old life were crushed that day as the second brain injury only compounded the effects of the gunshot wound. His once intermittent seizure disorder became extremely unstable, risking his safety. Furthermore, it had become apparent that John was incapable of performing the executive functions involved in leading a band, such as making performance dates, organizing shows, and more, and he irrationally lashed out at others when they disagreed with him. This wasn't the John his friends and family had known. There was no going back. The band dissolved.

> **FAST FACT**
>
> According to the Stanford School of Medicine, brain trauma caused by penetration of the brain (such as a bullet wound) results in epilepsy in 25–50 percent of cases.

You can still feel the sensitivity of an artist in John despite his cognitive and behavioral disabilities. He doesn't retain the memories of the person he was prior to his injuries, but a part of him will always dream of that boy who, he has been told, was the student-body president of his high school, sang in a rock band, and had such a bright future ahead of him brimming with the hope of youthful exuberance and invincibility.

Like other traumatically brain-injured people whose executive functions are impaired, John's symptoms demonstrated his inability to reflect on his own behavior and learn from the feedback given to him by others. Other symptoms associated with his dysfunctional obsessiveness, impulsiveness, and lack of empathy would have escalated if his family had not obtained guardianship of his affairs to protect him from his poor judgment and, specifically, from being exploited by others because of it. After assuming guardianship, his family exercised their court-appointed rights to readmit him to a well-established post-acute residential brain-injury center, despite his initial objections that he was "just fine and didn't need any help." . . .

John remained in his new treatment program for over a year, and during that time, with all the resources of a secure environment and an experienced interdisciplinary rehabilitation team working in his favor, his behavioral control improved. His OCD and depression responded to appropriate medications, and he became engaged in activities that provided him with a series of small successes that helped to rebuild his self-esteem and instill in him a desire to change, despite his difficulties in recognizing what actually had to change within himself. He gradually had therapeutic assignments with his family, at first in the neighboring community and then back at home, where he practiced behavioral strategies designed to help him psychically recognize when his anxiety or irritability began to escalate—before it got out of control.

A Therapist Diagnosed with Severe Mild Traumatic Brain Injury Struggles to Recover

Gail L. Denton

Gail L. Denton is a former psychotherapist and a survivor of mild traumatic brain injury (mTBI). She is the author of *Brainlash: Maximize Your Recovery from Mild Brain Injury*, works as an mTBI life coach, and hosts the website brainlash.com. In the following viewpoint, Denton describes her experience after suffering a concussion while inline skating with friends. She explains that after she was diagnosed with severe mild traumatic brain injury, she was told that because she scored high on the diagnostic tests, there was no help available to her. Frustrated by the limitations of Western science, she found her own path to healing, offering a message of hope to others recovering from brain injury.

SOURCE: Gail L. Denton, "Introduction," *Brainlash: Maximize Your Recovery from Mild Brain Injury*, 3rd ed., New York: Demos Medical Pub. 2008, p. 47. Copyright © 2008 by Demos Medical Publishing. All rights reserved. Reproduced by permission.

I wrote down what I was going through in order to trace my progress, to nurture my feelings of abandonment, and to try and make sense of a journey I had never thought to take or to even/ever prepare for. A journey of the mind. The road to recovery for mild brain damage, without so much as a bump on the head as a clue. A piece of the accident caused in part, it has been postulated, by the force of the blow to my abdomen (and the consequent Jell-O-like brain smashing into the inside of my skull because of the twisting nature of the fall—an internal whiplash) and the loss of oxygen to certain "less critical" parts of my brain due to heavy blood loss.

But because I wasn't a vegetable—because it wasn't catastrophic—because with my loss of brain power I still scored above average on the tests—they shrugged, patted me on the head, and told me to come back in two years for another test so they could measure my recovery. Two years can be a long time if your life is upside down, your personal mortgage banker lacks a similar sense of humor, and you probably need to make your way in the world between now and then.

Frustration with Western Medicine

I guess I'm angry. Not that Western science doesn't know what to do. They seem to know what to do for the catastrophically impaired. I've been a therapist for 15 years, and I don't remember ever telling someone to come back in two years so I could test their progress. No hints. No guidance. No clue.

"Your brain will generally gain maximum recovery in two years. Come back and we'll see how you do." And, by the way, your insurance company doesn't cover this neuropsychological test unless you have a prescription from the neurologist. Through some interesting loophole in the policy, the test is considered on the "psychology" side rather than the neurology side. A thousand dollars so someone can tell you what you've fairly well figured out for yourself in the first place or you wouldn't have gone to the neurologist.

Can't follow conversation, can't track sequential ideas, notice visual blind spots, can't tell jokes, laugh at jokes late, can't follow directions, can't add a short stack of numbers (like in the grocery store), get lost on the way to the office, don't recognize people, can't remember names, can't problem solve, cry at the drop of a hat, sex doesn't seem to work somehow, fail at following conversation and discussions with any sort of integrated or sequential theme, can't learn new information, need a map to go anywhere, blurt out inappropriate comments, overly sensitive to everything, get easily confused, very short attention span, lists and sticky notes become my daily lifesaver, get confused

For the author, using sticky notes as reminders of daily tasks to accomplish can be a lifesaver. (© Corbis Flirt/Alamy)

in traffic, can't recall details of my kids' lives, doubt my unimpaired intellect too, forget to rinse the shampoo out of my hair (it's a sequencing thing).

We called it my lumbar brain (should be limbic brain—a little anatomy humor). Journaling the changes seemed to build a trail of proof that I was healing.

Nontraditional Healing Systems

But the abandonment by my own profession infuriated me. How was I supposed to get from here to two years from here without any help? They looked blankly at me and suggested I return in two years. My injury wasn't very bad. I'd gradually get better to the extent of my potential (whatever that was) in that amount of time. I could pull myself up by my bootstraps (if I could find them), or do nothing, and my brain would or wouldn't get better. Thank you very much.

I postulated that if I could heal a broken leg, an ovarian cyst, and an 8-inch scar down the middle of my belly, those same principles had to apply to my brain.

Operating as a therapist was tough going. All the skills I needed to do my job were impaired. The listening, tracking, sequencing, and problem solving were mentally exhausting. But learning a new trade was out as well.

A PhD, with 20 years of business experience, 15 years of therapist experience, and nowhere to go. Trapped and abandoned. I went to nontraditional healing systems to seek new answers. Some answers existed in acupuncture, nutrition, herbs, visualization, behavioral optometry, cross-crawling, massage, cranial sacral manipulation, polarity therapy, chiropractic, psychological kinesiology, hypnosis, Pilates, astrology, and psychic energy work. The world of subtle energy science was of great value. I threw the non-Western book at myself. Did I gain more function than if I'd eaten pizza and watched MTV for two years? Who's to know?

I do know that my quality of life was improved, if simply because I felt active in my own recovery. If I thought anchovy milkshakes would have helped, I'd have drunk them, just for the pro-active benefit.

Dealing with Loss

Head-injury support groups were not for me. I didn't want to be a cliché. "How many Boulderites does it take to screw in a light bulb? Eight. They meet at dusk, form a support group, and learn to live with the darkness." I wasn't badly impaired. My impairment is known as "highly functional minimal loss." On the grand scale, I still had more marbles in my bag than most unimpaired folks, which is nice, I suppose. But it doesn't account for my loss. Discounts my loss, actually. I'm somewhere on the bell curve outside the sympathy line.

But *I* notice the loss. No, I *live* with the loss. I used to be smarter. I used to be a doctor. Now I'm a low-spark doctor. And I remember who I used to be and how I performed. There is devastating loss here for me. Who am I now? Where do I go from here? No map. No compass. No help. Not exactly caught in a creative moment. Not exactly equipped for self-extrication. Not exactly sure who I am, where I can go, who I'm going to be later, or what I'll do if I get where I'm going, wherever that is.

Feeling ethically challenged about going to the office, sitting under the shingle of my former self, charging big bucks, crossing my fingers, and hoping that no one runs screaming out the door, down the hall into the arms of one of the conveniently located barristers on the third floor.

Taking Responsibility for Recovery

A pain came with the vacuum that was the treatment model from Western medicine. No answers, and the

> **FAST FACT**
>
> According to a study published in the *Journal of Neurology, Neurosurgery & Psychiatry*, patients with negative beliefs about traumatic brain injury were significantly more likely to suffer from postconcussion syndrome.

condescending attitude really infuriated me. That icono-clastic attitude of "owners of the knowledge" combined with "kindly take your silly little problem down the hall" and don't bother us. It's all a tacky cover-up for a lack of answers, yet the need to own the territory nonetheless. Arrogance.

Arrogance is not an answer, a direction, or a therapy. Arrogance is not the truth. It is despicable, disrespect-ful, and inexcusable. I fought back. I will continue to take responsibility for my health. To look for additional answers to questions. To try and work out new ways to grow, change, and heal.

We all have an inner voice to guide us, whatever vol-ume yours happens to be. Listening to it is good. Follow-ing the advice is better still.

Pieces of me will be different. Other pieces of me are gone. New pieces of me are emerging. Discovering the new nooks and crannies is a frustrating, fascinating jour-ney. Mourning what's gone, welcoming what's new (even if it's the newest cowlick on the top of my head; if Alfalfa [a character in the old *Our Gang* TV series] can make it charming, so can I). Learning to love myself, today, each day, seems to be the final key to it all. Emerging from the pain, passing into the pleasure of this new being. "Space, the final frontier."

The Art of Graceful Recovery

Remember that you want to get well and all your physi-cal, emotional, and mental energy is focused to that end.

You shall prevail with love for yourself in a graceful, supportive manner.

Challenge exists for us today.

We improve daily, even in minute ways that reveal themselves slowly.

We heal daily.

It feels awkward, embarrassing, undignified, and devaluing to have this invisible struggle inside me.

I want my life back.

Notice you are alive, if slightly altered and inconvenienced.

This is a good place to start.

GLOSSARY

aphasia　A disorder characterized by either partial or total loss of the ability to communicate, either verbally or through written words. A person with aphasia may have difficulty speaking, reading, writing, recognizing the names of objects, or understanding what other people have said.

apoptosis　Also known as *programmed cell death*, a process controlled by the body in which a cell self-destructs and dies.

axon　A long threadlike structure neurons use to transmit information to one another via electical impulses.

blast injury　Physical trauma, including traumatic brain injury, resulting from an explosion.

caregiver burnout　Mental, emotional, and physical exhaustion resulting from neglecting one's own needs while caring for another.

chronic traumatic encephalopathy (CTE)　A progressive degenerative brain disease resulting from repetitive traumatic brain injury, such as multiple sports-related concussions.

closed head injury　A traumatic brain injury in which an object strikes the head or vice versa, but the skull is not fractured.

coma　A prolonged state of deep unconsciousness; may result from brain injury or be medically induced to aid healing.

computed tomography scan (CT)　A diagnostic technique in which the combined use of a computer and X-rays produces clear cross-sectional images of tissue. It provides clearer, more detailed information than X-rays alone.

computerized axial tomography (CAT)　*See* **computed tomography scan.**

concussion — A mild form of traumatic brain injury; a concussion usually involves a shifting of the brain inside the skull.

contrecoup injury — A brain injury located at the opposite side of the skull from the point of impact with an object.

coup injury — A brain injury located in the area where the head strikes or is struck by an object.

dementia pugilistica — *See* **chronic traumatic encephalopathy.**

diffuse axonal injury — Tearing of the nerve fibers (axons) that connect neurons in the brain, caused by sudden impact or rotational forces, as in a car accident.

electroencephalogram (EEG) — A record of the tiny electrical impulses produced by the brain's activity. By measuring characteristic wave patterns, the EEG can help diagnose certain conditions of the brain.

executive function — A group of cognitive abilities involved in planning and controlling behavior that is commonly affected by brain injury.

functional magnetic resonance imaging (fMRI) — A type of specialized magnetic resonance imaging that detects changes in the flow of blood in functioning brain areas.

Glasgow Coma Scale (GCS) — A clinical tool used to assess the level of consciousness in an individual with brain injury by precisely measuring vocal response, eye opening, and motor response.

intracranial pressure (ICP) — Pressure inside the skull that can increase dangerously following a brain injury due to brain swelling or a rise in cerebrospinal fluid (a clear liquid that cushions the brain and spinal cord).

locked-in syndrome — A rare condition, usually arising from brain injury or stroke, in which a person is conscious but completely paralyzed and unable to speak.

magnetic resonance imaging (MRI) — A diagnostic technique that provides high quality cross-sectional images of organs within the body without X-rays or other radiation.

minimally conscious state (MCS)	A condition of severely impaired consciousness distinct from persistent vegetative state or coma, in which a patient shows intermittent signs of consciousness.
neurocognitive stall	A condition affecting children with brain injuries, in which normal social, motor, and/or cognitive development slows down or stops.
neurologist	A physician specializing in treatment of diseases and injuries to the nerves, especially those of the central nervous system, which includes the brain and spinal cord.
neurons	Nerve and brain cells.
neuroplasticity	The brain's ability to compensate and recover from injury by forming new connections between neurons.
neurosurgeon	A physician specializing in brain and spine surgery.
neurotransmitter	Chemical substances produced within the body that are used by neurons to communicate with each other by relaying, modulating, or amplifying electrical signals.
pathologist	A physician specializing in determining the origin of disease; the pathologist usually conducts laboratory analyses of tissue and organs.
penetrating head injury	An injury in which an object breaks through the skull and enters the brain.
permanent vegetative state	*See* **persistent vegetative state.**
persistent vegetative state (PVS)	An ongoing condition resulting from severe brain damage in which the patient does not respond to physical or psychological stimuli.
positron-emission tomography (PET) scan	A computerized diagnostic technique that uses radioactive substances to examine structures of the body. When used to assess the brain, it produces a three-dimensional image that reflects the brain's metabolic and chemical activity.

postconcussion syndrome (PCS) A complex disorder occurring after a concussion that may persist for days, weeks, or months; various symptoms may occur, including dizziness, headaches, fatigue, and trouble concentrating.

posttraumatic amnesia (PTA) A period of time ranging from days to months after a brain injury, during which the patient is unable to recall new information.

second-impact syndrome (SIS) A condition that can afflict athletes and others who suffer successive concussions, occurring because their brains have not yet recovered from the initial concussions when they receive additional jolts.

second-shock syndrome *See* **second-impact syndrome.**

single photon emission computed tomography (SPECT) scan A computerized diagnostic technique that is similar to positron-emission tomography (PET). It produces lower-resolution images than PET does but is less expensive.

stem cell An undifferentiated or generic cell that can produce endless identical copies of itself as well as more specialized cells (such as brain cells).

subdural hematoma Bleeding inside the skull beneath the brain's protective membrane called the dura but not actually in the brain; hematomas can cause pressure inside the skull that can damage the brain.

substituted judgment A decision about medical care made on behalf of a patient no longer capable of making or communicating his or her own own decisions.

vegetative state *See* **persistent vegetative state.**

CHRONOLOGY

7000 B.C. Successful brain operations are performed in what is now France, as evidenced by surgical instruments found at an archaeological site.

3000 B.C. Brain surgery is practiced in Africa, according to papyrus writings from ancient Egypt. A word for "brain" is used in the writings for the first time in any language.

2000 B.C. Brain surgery is extensively practiced in pre-Incan civilization in present-day Peru to treat various medical conditions, including head injuries.

470–360 B.C. A number of influential texts on brain surgery are authored by famous Greek physician Hippocrates.

1st century A.D. In ancient Rome, Celsus describes brain injury symptoms in detail and operates on depressed skull fractures.

1848 In one of the most famous cases of traumatic brain injury (TBI), a US railroad construction accident sends a steel rod through foreman Phineas Gage's head, damaging his frontal lobes and causing significant personality changes.

1861 Neurologist Paul Broca theorizes that language function is located in a specific area of the brain, based on the study of two patients who had language problems following damage to that brain region. He preserves the brains of the two men and donates them to the Musée Dupuytren in Paris, France.

1914–1918 Soldiers in World War I receive traumatic brain injuries on an unprecedented scale from shrapnel, bullets, and blast injuries. Sir Gordon Holmes, an English neurologist, makes detailed observations of more than two thousand head injury cases.

1928 Pathologist Harrison S. Martland publishes his paper "Punch Drunk" in the *Journal of the American Medical Association*, describing for the first time the condition later known as chronic traumatic encephalopathy.

1937 US Navy surgeon J.A. Millspaugh coins the term *dementia pugilistica* to designate a condition of mental deterioration commonly observed in long-time boxers.

1940s The large number of soldiers surviving head wounds in World War II leads to a great deal of research into brain injury, much of which is still useful today, such as research on traumatic aphasia resulting from gunshot wounds to the head.

1957 Neurologist Macdonald Critchley publishes a study in the *British Medical Journal* in which he introduces the phrase *chronic progressive traumatic encephalopathy of boxers*. Later, this condition would become known as chronic traumatic encephalopathy.

1960s The mortality rate of those with severe traumatic brain injuries is about 90 percent.

1969 Britain's Royal College of Physicians publishes *Brain Damage in Boxers: A Study of the Prevalence of Traumatic Encephalopathy Among Ex-Professional Boxers* by A.H. Roberts, which states, "The accumulated sum total of these [brain] lesions, each perhaps of negligible importance in terms of function, may eventually produce a clinical syndrome bearing some resemblance to those in which there has been one severe traumatic episode causing diffuse destruction of cerebral axons."

1970s Computed tomography (CT) and magnetic resonance imaging (MRI) scanning are developed, leading to better TBI diagnoses. Fatality rates from TBI start to decline.

1972 Neurologist Fred Plum and neurosurgeon Bryan Jennett coin the term *persistent vegetative state*, describing it as a condition of "wakeful unresponsiveness" in which patients have no awareness of self or others even though their eyes are open.

1974 The *Lancet* publishes the Glasgow Coma Scale created by neurosurgeons Graham Teasdale and Bryan Jennett, which becomes a standard clinical tool used to assess a patient's level of consciousness using three simple tests of verbal response, eye opening, and motor response.

1977 J. Hume Adams and fellow researchers at the University of Glasgow publish a study in the journal *Brain* showing photographic evidence of diffuse axonal injury, which helps to explain TBI symptoms in people who have suffered concussions but do not appear to have significant head injury.

1983 Neurobiologist John Povlishock publishes a study in the *Journal of Neuropathology & Experimental Neurology* that demonstrates microscopic damage in the brains of patients with mild TBI, proving that concussions cause detectable damage to the brain.

1984 An article in the *Journal of the American Medical Association* introduces "second-impact syndrome," which refers to the serious effects of multiple concussions that occur within a short period of time.

1986 The *Physician and Sports Medicine* publishes Robert Cantu's guidelines for medical personnel and coaches to determine under what circumstances, and for how long, sports players need to be removed from play after suffering concussions.

1989 The American Academy of Neurology defines the term *persistent vegetative state* in a position paper, offering the opinion that such patients do not feel pain.

1990s The "Decade of the Brain" is declared by US president George H.W. Bush "to enhance public awareness of the benefits to be derived from brain research."

1990 The Individuals with Disabilities Education Act (IDEA), a federal law protecting the rights of disabled students, is enacted; it includes traumatic brain injury as a specific category.

1992 The Defense and Veterans Head Injury Program, a joint venture of the US Department of Defense and the US Department of Veterans Affairs (VA), is founded during the Persian Gulf War to coordinate TBI education, research, and care throughout veteran and military care systems. Later, the name is changed to Defense and Veterans Brain Injury Center (DVBIC).

1994 Using modern computer imaging, neuroscientist Hanna Damasio creates a detailed three-dimensional image of railroad foreman Gage's brain based on photographs of his skull, confirming that the iron rod that passed through his brain in 1848 missed his language and motor centers but destroyed regions involved in rational decision making, planning, and sociability.

1996   The term *chronic traumatic encephalopathy* is introduced to the medical literature in a paper by neuropathologist Ann C. McKee et al. and becomes the preferred medical term to describe dementia caused by cumulative brain injury in athletes.

1997   Drs. Barry D. Jordan, Norman Relkin, and colleagues discover that boxers with a gene mutation called apoE4, previously linked with a significantly increased chance of developing Alzheimer's disease, were much more likely to suffer from dementia pugilistica, to have more severe symptoms, and to suffer the condition from a younger age—suggesting that some people have a genetic disposition toward chronic traumatic encephalopathy.

2000   The National Institute of Neurological Disorders and Stroke (NINDS) is authorized by the Congressional Children's Health Act to carry out and support traumatic brain injury research aimed at creating rehabilitative behavioral and cognitive therapies.

2001   Traumatic brain injury is widely viewed as the "signature wound" of the war in Afghanistan (and, later, also in Iraq). Increased attention is focused on the problem, advancing treatment and rehabilitation.

2002   The American Academy of Neurology publishes a paper distinguishing *minimally conscious state* (MCS) from *coma* and *vegetative state*, noting inconsistent but detectable signs of consciousness in MCS patients. The authors advise caregivers that the patient "should be treated with dignity, and caregivers should be cognizant of the patient's potential for understanding and perception of pain."

2005   The Polytrauma and Blast-Related Injury Quality Enhancement Research Initiative is founded by the VA to further the goal of rehabilitation for veterans with blast-related injuries, including TBI.

2007   The VA starts to screen all veterans of the wars in Afghanistan and Iraq for TBI.

Speech and language expert Nina Dronkers and a team of researchers at the University of California–Davis perform an MRI scan of the two brains preserved by Dr. Broca in 1861, creating a detailed map of the damaged areas.

2009   Neurosurgeon Douglas Smith publishes a study in the *Journal of Neuroscience* proving that axons can suffer as much damage by being lightly stretched twice as they can by being strongly stretched once and detailing the mechanisms that create increased vulnerability following the first stretch. His research highlights the danger of serious brain injury resulting from a series of relatively minor concussions.

Neuropathologist McKee discovers chronic traumatic encephalopathy in an eighteen-year-old male who had received multiple concussions playing high school football, the youngest known case of the condition. She describes her findings as "highly alarming" and "something you should never see in an eighteen-year-old brain."

Trendsetting legislation known as the Zackery Lystedt Law is passed in Washington state requiring young athletes to be removed immediately from play when a concussion is suspected and not allowed to return until a qualified health care professional gives written permission.

2010   A National Football League (NFL) athlete named Chris Henry, who died at age twenty-six, is found by Dr. Bennet Omalu to have suffered from chronic traumatic encephalopathy, further demonstrating that the condition is not confined to retired professionals of middle age and beyond, but can affect younger athletes as well.

The NFL widely distributes a poster warning of the dangers of concussion to athletes, which states that concussions "may lead to problems with memory and communication, personality changes, as well as depression and the early onset of dementia" and that "concussions and conditions resulting from repeated brain injury can change your life and your family's life forever."

The Centers for Disease Control and Prevention (CDC) reports that 1.7 million people in the United States have a traumatic brain injury each year, of which 52,000 (about 3 percent) die. Approximately 80 percent, or 1.365 million, are treated in an emergency room and released. The report also states that 30.5 percent of all injury-related deaths have TBI as a contributing factor.

ORGANIZATIONS TO CONTACT

The editors have compiled the following list of organizations concerned with the issues debated in this book. The descriptions are derived from materials provided by the organizations. All have publications or information available for interested readers. The list was compiled on the date of publication of the present volume; the information provided here may change. Be aware that many organizations take several weeks or longer to respond to inquiries, so allow as much time as possible.

AbleData
8630 Fenton St.,
Ste. 930
Silver Spring, MD
20910
(301) 608-8998: toll-free:
(800) 227-0216
fax: (301) 608-8958
e-mail: abledata@
macrointernational
.com
website: www.abledata
.com

AbleData provides objective information on assistive technology and rehabilitation equipment available from domestic and international sources to consumers, organizations, professionals, and caregivers within the United States. Almost forty thousand products are listed in twenty categories such as "Aids for daily living," "Communication," "Computers," and "Walking."

American Association of Neurological Surgeons (AANS)
5550 Meadowbrook Dr.
Rolling Meadows, IL
60008-3852
(847) 378-0500; toll-free: (888) 566-2267
fax: (847) 378-0600
e-mail: info@aans.org
website: www.aans.org

Representing doctors who specialize in brain surgery, the AANS promotes neurosurgery as a science and publishes the *Journal of Neurosurgery,* which contains articles outlining the latest advances in brain surgery. Visitors to the organization's website can find statistics about neurosurgery, news reports about brain injuries, and press releases outlining AANS's efforts to advance the science of neurosurgery.

Bicycle Helmet Safety Institute
4611 Seventh St. South
Arlington, VA 22204-1419
(703) 486-0100
e-mail: info@helmets.org
website: www.bhsi.org

The Bicycle Helmet Safety Institute is an organization that serves as an advocate for the use of bicycle helmets by all riders. Visitors to the organization's website can find extensive information on how to select a helmet, which states require riders to wear helmets, and statistics on head injuries sustained by riders who do not wear helmets. Free publications include pamphlets and an e-mail newsletter, *Helmet Update*.

Brain Injury Association of America (BIAA)
1608 Spring Hill Rd., Ste. 110
Vienna, VA 22182
(703) 761-0750
fax: (703) 761-0755
e-mail: info@biusa.org
website: www.biausa.org

The BIAA serves as an advocacy group for brain-injury patients and their families. The group has helped win government grants for research and rehabilitation projects and has published guides for families and others whose lives are touched by traumatic brain injuries. Visitors to the association's website can read stories of how brain-injury patients endured their rehabilitation, access information on living with brain injury, sign up for the organization's mailing list, request specific information, participate in a forum, or learn about upcoming educational events. BIAA also publishes the *Challenge!*, a quarterly magazine featuring news from Capitol Hill and across the country.

BrainLine.org
WETA
2775 S. Quincy St.
Arlington, VA 22206
(703) 998-2020
e-mail: info@brainline.org
website: www.brainline.org

BrainLine is a national multimedia project funded by the Defense and Veterans Brain Injury Center. It offers information and resources about preventing, treating, and living with traumatic brain injury. The organization serves people with brain injury, their families, and professionals in the field. BrainLine provides a series of webcasts, an electronic newsletter, and an extensive outreach campaign in partnership with national organizations concerned about traumatic brain injury.

Brain Trauma Foundation
7 World Trade Center, 34th Fl.
250 Greenwich St.
New York, NY 10007
(212) 772-0608
website: www.brain
trauma.org

The Brain Trauma Foundation was established to support medical research and provide education to physicians about traumatic brain injury (TBI). Visitors to the foundation's website can find statistics about TBI in the United States, information on TBI in the military, recorded webinars, and an archive of news articles about the latest developments in brain trauma research.

Centers for Disease Control and Prevention (CDC)
1600 Clifton Rd.
Atlanta, GA 30333
(800) 232-4636
e-mail: cdcinfo@cdc
.gov
website: www.cdc.gov

As the federal government's chief public health agency, the CDC explores trends in diseases and other conditions that affect the health of Americans. The National Center for Injury Prevention and Control, an agency of the CDC, maintains an extensive archive of information on traumatic brain injury at www.cdc.gov/TraumaticBrainInjury/index.html.

Defense and Veterans Brain Injury Center (DVBIC)
11300 Rockville Pike, Ste. 1100
Rockville, MD 20852
(866) 966-1020
website: http://dvbic
.org

The DVBIC exists to serve active-duty military personnel, their beneficiaries, and veterans with traumatic brain injuries (TBIs) through state-of-the-art clinical care, innovative clinical research initiatives, and educational programs. DVBIC fulfills this mission through ongoing collaboration with military, Veterans Administration, and civilian health partners, local communities, families, and individuals with TBIs. Its website offers a variety of information and resources for patients and caregivers, including the e-mail newsletter *Brainwaves*.

**National Institute
of Mental Health
(NIMH)**
Science Writing, Press,
and Dissemination
Branch
6001 Executive Blvd.,
Rm. 8184, MSC 9663
Bethesda, MD 20892-
9663
(866) 615-6464
e-mail: nimhinfo@nih
.gov
website: www.nimh.nih
.gov

NIMH is the federal government's chief funding agency for
mental health research in America and a member of the National Institutes of Health. The organization's website offers a
wealth of information on the brain, as well as on mental illness-
es caused by traumatic brain injury, including depression and
attention-deficit disorder. Its publications include fact sheets,
booklets, and brochures.

**National Institute
of Neurological
Disorders and Stroke
(NINDS)**
PO Box 5801
Bethesda, MD 20824
(301) 496-5751; toll-
free: (800) 352-9424
website: www.ninds
.nih.gov

NINDS is an agency of the National Institutes of Health whose
mission is to reduce the burden of neurological disease, including brain injury and stroke. To this end it conducts, fosters,
coordinates, and guides research on the causes, prevention,
diagnosis, and treatment of neurological disease and supports
basic research in related scientific areas. Visitors to the agency's
website can find a description of traumatic brain injury (TBI),
explanation of methods of treatment and rehabilitation, and the
status of research into the causes of TBI.

**Sports Legacy
Institute**
PO Box 181225
Boston, MA 02118
(781) 262-3324
e-mail: info@sports
legacy.org
website: www.sports
legacy.org

The Sports Legacy Institute is an organization established by
former college football player and pro wrestler Chris Nowinski,
an advocate for athletes who suffer from traumatic brain injury,
and Robert Cantu, an expert on brain injury. Its mission is to
solve the concussion crisis in sports and the military through
medical research, treatment, and education and prevention. The
institute offers an e-mail newsletter, an archive of news articles
and video about concussions, updates on recent brain injury
research, and information on how the families of deceased athletes can donate their brain tissue to medical research.

ThinkFirst National Injury Prevention Foundation
1801 N. Mill St., Ste. F
Naperville, IL 60563
(630) 961-1400; toll-free: (800) 844-6556
fax: (630) 961-1401
e-mail: thinkfirst@thinkfirst.org
website: www.thinkfirst.org

The ThinkFirst National Injury Prevention Foundation, formerly known as the National Head and Spinal Cord Injury Prevention Program, was founded in 1986. ThinkFirst programs educate young people about their personal vulnerability to traumatic injury and the importance of making safe choices. The organization provides health professionals with training, tools, and support to assist local chapters in spreading the prevention message in their communities. Its website has different information sections for children and youth of various ages. ThinkFirst publishes a newsletter, *Prevention Pages.*

FOR FURTHER READING

Books

Jean-Dominique Bauby, *The Diving Bell and the Butterfly: A Memoir of Life in Death*. New York: Vintage, 2007.

Walter G. Bradley, *Treating the Brain*. New York: Dana, 2009.

Linda Carroll and David Rosner, *The Concussion Crisis: Anatomy of a Silent Epidemic*. New York: Simon & Schuster, 2011.

John W. Cassidy and Karla Dougherty, *Mindstorms: The Complete Guide for Families Living with Traumatic Brain Injury*. Cambridge, MA: Da Capo, 2009.

Audrey Daisley, Rachel Tams, and Udo Kischka, *Head Injury: The Facts*. Oxford: Oxford University Press, 2009.

Gail L. Denton, *Brainlash: Maximize Your Recovery from Mild Brain Injury*. 3rd ed. New York: Demos Medical, 2008.

Norman Doidge, *The Brain That Changes Itself: Stories of Personal Triumph from the Frontiers of Brain Science*. New York: Penguin, 2007.

Carolyn E. Dolen, *Brain Injury Rewiring for Loved Ones: A Lifeline to New Connections*. Enumclaw, WA: Idyll Arbor, 2010.

Joseph J. Fins, "Brain Injury: The Vegetative and Minimally Conscious States." In *Bioethics Briefing Book*. Garrison, NY: The Hastings Center, 2008.

Gabrielle D. Giffords and Mark E. Kelly, *Gabby: A Story of Courage and Hope*. New York: Scribner, 2011.

Geo Gosling, *TBI Purgatory: Comes After Being in TBI Hell*. Parker, CO: Outskirts, 2010.

Robert S. Gotlin, ed., *Sports Injuries Guidebook: Athletes' and Coaches' Resource for Identification, Treatment and Recovery*. Champaign, IL: Human Kinetics, 2008.

Beth Jameson and Larry Jameson, *Brain Injury Survivor's Guide: Welcome to Our World.* Denver: Outskirts, 2008.

Rahul Jandial, Charles B. Newman, and Samuel A. Hughes, *100 Questions & Answers About Head and Brain Injuries.* Sudbury, MA: Jones and Bartlett, 2009.

Michael Paul Mason, *Head Cases: Stories of Brain Injury and Its Aftermath.* New York: Farrar, Straus & Giroux, 2008.

Garry Prowe, *Successfully Surviving a Brain Injury: A Family Guidebook; From the Emergency Room to Selecting a Rehabilitation Facility.* Gainesville, FL: Brain Injury Success, 2010.

Cheryle Sullivan, *Brain Injury Survival Kit: 365 Tips, Tools, & Tricks to Deal with Cognitive Function Loss.* New York: Demos Medical, 2008.

Felise S. Zollman, *Manual of Traumatic Brain Injury Management.* New York: Demos Medical, 2011.

Periodicals and Internet Sources

Tom Avril, "Researchers Seek New Tools to Flag Concussions," *Philadelphia Inquirer*, October 5, 2010. http://articles.philly.com /2010-10-05/news/24976722_1_brain-cells-concussions-chronic -traumatic-encephalopathy.

Andrew Bast, "The Warrior's Brain," *The Daily Beast*, November 11, 2010. www.thedailybeast.com/newsweek/2010/11/08/ veteran-s-head-injuries-confound-military-doctors.html.

Deborah Blum, "Will Science Take the Field?," *New York Times*, February 5, 2010.

Bruce Bower, "Self-Serve Brains: Personal Identity Veers to the Right Hemisphere," *Science News*, February 11, 2006. http://bio psychiatry.com/misc/personal-identity.html.

Peter J. Boyer, "What's Really Going on with Gabby Giffords?," *Newsweek*, April 18 2011. www.thedailybeast.com/newsweek /2011/04/10/what-s-really-going-on-with-gabby-giffords .html.

Raf Casert, "Rom Houben, Man in Coma for 23 Years, Was Fully Conscious, Mom Says," *Huffington Post*, November 23, 2009. www.huffingtonpost.com/2009/11/23/rom-houben-man -in-coma-fo_n_367798.html.

Bill Coffin, "Tragic Tale," LifeHealthPro, November 7, 2011. www.lifehealthpro.com/2011/11/07/tragic-tale.

Mo Costandi, "The Incredible Case of Phineas Gage," *Neurophilosophy* (blog), July 6, 2007. http://scienceblogs.com/neuro philosophy/2007/07/the_incredible_case_of_phineas.php.

————, "Unusual Penetrating Brain Injuries," *Neurophilosophy* (blog), May 22, 2008. http://scienceblogs.com/neurophilosophy/2008/05/unusual_penetrating_brain_injuries.php.

Joely P. Esposito et al., "Traumatic Brain Injury: Emotional Sequelae in Children and Adolescents," *Pediatrics for Parents*, January 2008. www.pedsforparents.com/articles/3329.shtml.

David H. Gorski, "Update on the Case of 'Coma Man' Rom Houben: Facilitated Communication Is Still Woo," *Respectful Insolence* (blog), February 15, 2010. http://scienceblogs.com/insolence/2010/02/update_on_the_case_of_coma_man_rom_hoube.php.

Cathy Gulli, "Concussions: They're Not Just for Men Anymore: Mounting Research Shows Concussion Rates Are a Lot Higher in Female than Male Athletes—Even in 'Safer' Sports," *Maclean's*, June 17, 2011. www2.macleans.ca/2011/06/17/blind sided/.

————, "The Damage Done by Concussions: Sidney Crosby Is a Case Study in What We Know, and What We Don't Know About Concussions," *Maclean's*, February 4, 2011. www2.macleans.ca/2011/02/04/the-damage-done/.

Harriet Hall, "Thoughts on Neuroplasticity," Science-Based Medicine, March 18, 2008. www.sciencebasedmedicine.org/index.php/thoughts-on-neuroplasticity/.

Virginia Hughes, "Breaking Through," *The Last Word on Nothing* (blog), November 29, 2011. www.lastwordonnothing.com/2011/11/29/breaking-through/.

Jeneen Interlandi, "A Drug That Wakes the Near Dead," *New York Times*, December 1, 2011. www.nytimes.com/2011/12/04/magazine/can-ambien-wake-minimally-conscious.html?page wanted=all.

Elizabeth Landau, "The Brain's Amazing Potential for Recovery," CNN, May 5, 2011. www.cnn.com/2011/HEALTH/05/05 /brain.plasticity.giffords/index.html.

Jessica Leeder, "'Talk and Die Syndrome' Made Actress's Death Difficult to Prevent," *Globe & Mail* (Toronto), March 20, 2009. www.theglobeandmail.com/news/national/talk-and-die-syndrome -made-actresss-death-difficult-to-prevent/article1150182/.

Steve Maich, "The Concussion Time Bomb," *Maclean's*, October 22, 2007. www.macleans.ca/science/health/article.jsp?content=2 0071022_110256_110256&page=1.

Michael Mason, "Dead Men Walking," *Discover*, February 23, 2007. http://discovermagazine.com/2007/mar/dead-men-walk ing/article_view?b_start:int=0&-C=.

T. Christian Miller, Daniel Zwerdling, Susanne Reber, and Robin Fields, "Brain Wars: How the Military Is Failing Its Wounded," Dart Center for Journalism & Trauma, April 14, 2011. http://dartcenter.org/content/brain-injuries-remain -undiagnosed-in-thousands-soldiers.

Neuroskeptic (blog), "Neuroplasticity Revisited," June 16, 2011. http://neuroskeptic.blogspot.com/2011/06/neuroplasticity-re visited.html.

Craig J. Phillips, "Traumatic Brain Injury and Denial—My Perspective as a TBI Survivor," *Second Chance to Live* (blog), May 12, 2007. http://secondchancetolive.wordpress.com/2007/05/12 /traumatic-brain-injury-and-denial-my-perspective-as-a-tbi -survivor/.

Alan Schwarz, "As Injuries Rise, Scant Oversight for Football Helmet Safety," *New York Times*, October 21, 2010. www.ny times.com/2010/10/21/sports/football/21helmets.html?_r=1 &pagewanted=all.

———, "Study Says Brain Trauma Can Mimic A.L.S.," *New York Times*, August 17, 2010. www.nytimes.com/2010/08/18 /sports/18gehrig.html?pagewanted=all.

Michael E. Selzer, "Harnessing the Brain's Power to Adapt After Injury," The DANA Foundation, November 6, 2007. www.dana .org/news/cerebrum/detail.aspx?id=9996.

Gordy Slack, "Turning to Software to Help Treat Brain Injuries," *New York Times*, June 17, 2011. www.nytimes.com/2011/06/17/us/17bcbrain.html.

Janice Turner, "That Deep Maternal Urge . . . to Kill Your Child; If a Coma Patient Can Be Denied Sustenance, Why Should the Woman Who Injected Her Brain-Damaged Son Be Criminalized?," *Times* (London), January 23, 2010.

Kelly Whiteside, "Concussions No Fun, Take Toll on School for Injured Athletes," *USA Today*, December 28, 2010. www.usatoday.com/sports/2010-12-27-concussion-cover-brianna-binowski_N.htm.

INDEX